H
USE
Your
SELLING POWER

by
WALTER HORVATH

PRENTICE-HALL, INC.
Englewood Cliffs, N.J. 07632

BY THE SAME AUTHOR

Twelve Guides to Modern Salesmanship
How's Your Selling Technique?
Guided Study Course in Salesmanship
Six Successful Selling Techniques

Library of Congress Cataloging in Publication Data
Horvath, Walter Julius.
    How to use your selling power.

    Includes index.
    1. Selling.   I. Title.
[HF5438.25.H67   1982]   658.8'5   81-21135
ISBN 0-13-437087-2 {PBK}   AACR2

CONTENTS

A WORD FROM THE PUBLISHER

Walter Horvath's sales training materials have made a profound impression on the salesmanship of our age.

Thousands of salesmen have found in them the "credo" that leads to progress; sales managers from coast to coast have adopted them as their program of salesmen's training and stimulation. They are used by companies such as RCA Victor, Fuller Brush, Eastern Air Lines, The Borden Company, Remington Rand, Ward Baking, Squibb, Underwood, and hundreds of others; by leading colleges and universities; by the Armed Forces for training of recruiting personnel. Distribution has been international, and has run into the millions.

Now, in this new edition, the Horvath materials are made available in bound-book form. Readers will find in this volume the same practical guidance that has always distinguished the author's famous messages. But they will also find more. For Walter Horvath, in preparing HOW TO USE YOUR SELLING POWER, has made of it more than a *book;* yes, even more than an organized course of study or instruction. He has made it possible for this book to be used as an actual *field* tool—to be used by the salesman for the solution of problems as he is about to *face* them in his hour-by-hour selling activities.

How this has been accomplished is explained in Chapter 2.

We think this work marks still a new milestone, an even greater contribution, than what has gone before.

We present Walter Horvath's first bound book with great pleasure, and with some pride.

THE PUBLISHER

1

THE MOST IMPORTANT FACT
IN SALESMANSHIP

Through the years innumerable people have asked me, "What is the most important single thing that a salesman should know?"

Invariably and without hesitation, my reply is: "The most important fact in salesmanship is that there is a solution to every single problem in selling, *if only you can find it.*"

Once a salesman grasps that fundamental fact, he becomes a better and stronger man. He will not sell every prospect; he will not avoid all mistakes; he will not, in short, turn in a perfect score. But he will make many sales that he would otherwise lose, for the mere understanding that there *is* a solution urges him on to seek it, when another man would decide that there is nothing further he can do.

In the pages that follow you will find a discussion of each type of problem that can confront you, or anyone, in selling. You will find problems that arise from prospects' "closed minds," or other forms of resistance; problems resulting from the salesman's failure to do and say the right thing at the right time; problems arising from all the other circumstances that so often lose the sale.

To all these problems you will find the answer.

No book, no sales manager, no system of training can make

any salesman *apply* the right solution to any selling problem. Intelligent application is a responsibility that always has rested, and necessarily must rest, on the salesman himself.

But as long as there are goods and services to sell and prospects to whom they must be sold, the "star" will always be the man who somehow seeks out the answers to his problems and then proceeds to *apply* them.

Your selling problems, whatever they may be, are examined within the covers of this book. If any salesman were able properly to apply all the points that this book suggests, in all his work, that man would be the world's first perfect salesman.

Those who seek to top the field, those who wish to improve their selling score, those who want to probe the concrete evidence of the all-important principle that there *is* an answer to every selling problem: This book is intended particularly for you.

The world belongs to those who have the capacity to grow. In salesmanship, growth consists in finding better ways of meeting the problems that confront all who sell. If this book helps you solve but one of your own unsolved problems, it will have repaid you for reading it, and me for writing it. If it does not, why, either you or I have failed!

2

THERE'S ONE SURE ROAD
TO SUCCESS

You are a salesman. Success, for you, is therefore a matter of reaching your maximum selling power. Perhaps in your case that means an increase of 10 per cent, or 25 per cent. Perhaps it is 100 per cent, or more.

The question is both practical and important, for your answer will determine just how you will use this guidebook. Here are the alternatives. Only you can select the one that satisfies your needs. If you are realistic, if you select the method that is appropriate in your case, you have then started down the one sure road to success.

1. Simply read through Chapters 3 to 20. These are actual case histories of the solution of selling problems. You will find them interesting, instructive, stimulating.

2. Fill out with some care the "True-False Quiz" that appears at the end of each of these chapters. You'll enjoy scoring yourself, but there's much more to it than that. Many a salesman (including some mighty good ones!) have found in this step a golden nugget that has "paid off" for them, year after year.

3. Take this guidebook *out in the field,* and make it *work* for you!

How? The answer to that question is Chapter 21. Suppose

you have reason to think that on your next call you may run into some tough objections. In Chapter 21 you'll find a very brief, ultra-convenient *summary* of all that's in this guidebook on that subject. (You'll find other summaries there too, on closing, presentation, how to find prospects, how to lick a slump, and a checklist of good selling habits. So whether it's "objections" or one of these other topics you want to brush up on quickly, turn to Chapter 21.)

It would take you a long time to build such a summary yourself. It's been done *for* you. Of course, these summaries will not mean much to you unless you have read the preceding chapters. But if you have, you will find in Chapter 21 a source of extra selling power that may, overnight, make you a "star." It has happened, to men pretty much like you and me.

4. Success may require one final step. From time to time you may want to review specific points in Chapters 3 to 20. Not just in outline-reminder form, as in Chapter 21, but the whole story. There is no need to reread the whole book merely to review the subject you have in mind. Simply turn to Chapter 22. Here you will find a practical breakdown of the elements of salesmanship. Find the one you are interested in, and turn to the references indicated.

Yes, there is one sure road to success. Only you can find it, and only you can decide to follow it. Only you are responsible if you fail to use the help available to take you where you want to go.

3

YOU CAN'T SELL IF YOU
CAN'T CLOSE

"Meet Bill Blake"

"There goes the world's greatest closer," remarked a friend of mine one day. "He's Bill Blake, and say, you should see him close the real *tough* ones with his *hat trick!*"

Well, I thought I knew a thing or two about closing, but here was a *new* wrinkle. So I asked my friend, who happened to be Bill's sales manager, to explain.

"If you really want to know about Blake's technique," he countered, "why not tag along with him on a few calls?"

And so it was arranged. Bill and I started out together the next morning, and I must admit I felt that at least *I* wasn't wasting my time when it developed that our very first prospect was going to be about as tough as they come.

Hats Off to Bill!

For ten minutes I sat in rapt attention as Bill skillfully met objection after objection, and in the process converted a man who was *positive* he wasn't interested into one who said he certainly wanted to consider the matter, and could Blake come back in about a week?

Now that in itself was quite a victory, but it wasn't enough for a battler like Bill Blake! So he made three or four more stabs at a close, and each one carried a real wallop, but Mr. Prospect just wouldn't decide then and there.

And then, at the exact point where further "pushing" would have been out of order, Bill went and *did* it. He reached for his hat, picked up his briefcase, got up from his chair, meanwhile cordially thanking the prospect for his time and courtesy. And when Mr. Prospect had assured us that he was glad we'd called, Bill said, "Yes, I'm certain it's been a profitable visit. And before I go, do you mind if I ask one question?"

"No indeed," said our friend, relaxed and almost expansive now that the issue was settled.

"Wouldn't it save us all a lot of time," asked Bill, in a casual sort of way, "if you were to okay the deal now, with the privilege of canceling within one week if you *should* decide otherwise?"

Two minutes later we were outside, with the order safely signed, *without any cancellation clause*. By "reaching for his hat," Bill had achieved much more than an opportunity to try once more for a close; he was able to get in this final "lick" at the one point in the *whole* interview when the prospect's guard was *down*.

Strong Salesmen Are Strong Closers

Now, that was as fine an exhibition of closing technique as I've ever seen. Nothing under the sun could have won that particular order on that particular day, except Bill's "hat trick."

But don't get the idea that Blake used only one method of closing! Before lunch I saw him "go through his paces" with several other prospects, and the only thing these interviews had in common was this: *Bill was a strong closer!*

Of course, every good salesman is a strong closer. I have learned to place closing ability at the very top of my list of musts for any type of selling, retail, wholesale, or what have you.

Because there's something special about closing, you may be interested to know how I like to think about it. Suppose there were a horse race with six entrants. Suppose two ran almost neck-and-neck, far outdistancing the others. Well, there'd be a lot of applause for the one who lost by a nose. "There's a hoss to watch," people would say.

Selling Isn't a Horse Race

But what happens when it comes to selling? If six salesmen (or saleswomen) have a go at the same prospect (or shopper), the minute one of them closes the sale, each of the other five has lost that sale with equal finality. If one of them almost landed the order, but didn't, he's in exactly the same boat as the one who made the poorest try. So I'm going to try to give you all the practical help I can on closing.

Now if I were limited to just one single piece of advice on this important topic, I know just what it would be. It has been my privilege to observe some hundreds of salesmen in their actual sales work, and they've ranged "all over the lot" as to type, age, experience, and so on. Excluding the top-notch closers, who obviously didn't need any advice on this subject, I've had to tell all of them the same thing: "You don't begin to close early enough; you don't keep on closing long enough; and you don't try enough closes between your first and your last."

Just to show you that this is a completely practical bit of advice, let me give you a quick (and perhaps an extreme) example of how it works.

If You Can't Open—Close!

Some years ago I stopped at a garage in a busy little Ohio town to have some work done on my car. The garage man knew I was in a hurry, so when a salesman stopped in, he gave him a quick brushoff: "Too busy right now. Got a rush job." And he kept right on working.

"Well, what I want to tell you will take only a minute," pleaded the salesman.

"Nope—ain't got a minute to listen right now." And that was that.

Twice more within the next hour exactly the same thing took place. Three salesmen in a row had been turned down without a chance to tell their story. But number four got a hearing, and an order! Why? Simply because he was a strong closer! In fact, he countered the "brushoff" with a close!

But perhaps I'd better tell you the whole story. This chap, "Number Four," walked in and said, just about like the others, "Mr. Jones, my name is Smith, representing the Brown Company."

Jones said, as before, "Too busy right now. Got a rush job." And he kept on working.

Smith Rings the Bell

Now watch carefully. Did Smith argue the point about time, about getting a quick minute when the prospect was busy? No, sir, not that lad! He was too smart to waste his last shot!

What he said was, "O. K., suppose I send you one of our new 'Fixall Kits'? You need it!"

Well, Jones stopped working. For the first time in an hour he even glanced at a salesman. "What's a 'Fixall Kit'?" he asked, more suspicious than interested.

"Every garage in town has ordered one today," said Smith, talking fast as he reeled off some names. "And I'll rush yours, too, so that you'll have yours at the same time as they do!" (Another close!)

"Now wait a minute, feller!" Jones by this time was aware of but one single thing in the whole world: Salesman Smith! The fact that he had a "rush job" was completely forgotten. The monkey wrench he had been plying was now out of his hand. Even before he spoke again I had guessed about what he would say.

"Now just what is this kit that everybody's buying?"

You see, this time he was demanding the story with a vigor equal to his refusal to listen in the three previous cases.

All this happened years ago, but I remember as though it were yesterday how I figured that Smith had earned himself a cool ten or 15 dollars in as many minutes.

Close Early, Often, and Late

Again I say, nothing under the sun but superb closing technique could have landed that particular order at that time. Yes, it pays to close early—and late. And make no mistake about it: It pays to close often!

Now when I was cutting my eyeteeth in selling, there was a lot of to-do about this magic thing called "the psychological moment." Salesmen of all types believed in it implicitly. The idea was that there was one, and only one, supreme moment in an interview when it was smart to go into a close.

Double Trouble

If you closed too early, ran the theory, you'd get a "No."

That was bad. If you closed too late, you had missed your big chance, and you might as well pack up and make tracks for your next prospect.

What a prolific source of alibis that old theory was. "The phone rang just at the psychological moment," or, "Right at the psychological moment a big customer was announced, so we were interrupted."

Well, today we know better. Granted that there may well be some point in an interview when the buyer's interest is at its very height, and granted that a really smart salesman may be able to "spot" this moment accurately, what's so smart about putting all your eggs in one basket? The fact that you've tried a few closes before that "moment" arrives won't keep you from trying again at that time, provided, of course, you haven't bungled your earlier attempts.

Similarly, the fact that you've missed the close at the "psychological moment" shouldn't keep you from trying again—and trying and trying as long as the interview lasts.

Champions Don't Lick Themselves

Now the best way I know of to clarify this all-important point is to draw an analogy between selling and boxing.

I'd be sorry for the boxer whose strategy was never to let go with his right except at that one supreme moment when he felt he had the greatest chance of scoring a knockout. I feel equally sorry for the salesman who is the victim of an identical "one-blow" selling strategy.

And I think it's pretty obvious why there are many salesmen who fall into that category. The reason is that they are *afraid* of a "no." And they're afraid of it because they don't know how to keep the interview going once the word is spoken.

Well, the reason they don't know how is because they themselves give to their attempt to close a degree of finality that it needn't possess at all.

Try, Try Again

Let's put it this way. Salesman White, a skillful closer, makes a "trial close" two minutes after the interview begins. He realizes it is a trial close; he knows in advance that there is a relatively slight chance that it will evoke an instant "O. K." Of course, if it does, he has won. But if it doesn't, he's neither nonplussed nor at a loss for an immediate resumption of the interview. He knows that the prospect realizes that he has only begun his talk; that the prospect expects him to carry on. So in another minute or so, he tries again; and so on during the entire interview.

Now neither this multiple closing technique nor anything else will make a successful salesman out of a man who lacks all finesse or skill in selling. A bungler ought to be afraid of a trial close, since he will probably handle it in such a way as to get a "No" in reply, and one that does have the finality that he fears!

Nine Out of Ten Win

But 90 per cent of us who make our living by selling can use this method to real advantage if we will but understand what goes on in the prospect's mind as we proceed. He isn't saying to himself, "Well, Mr. Salesman, you were entitled to just one request that I buy, and here you've used it up already, so be on your way."

No, he is busy doing something that is of tremendous help and value to you.

Make Your Prospect Work For You

Your prospect, responding to your trial close, has probably told you more or less exactly why he is turning you down. "No, it's too expensive," or, "No, I want to see what your competitors have to offer," or some other reasoned answer is the reward for a workmanlike trial close that doesn't win a "yes."

I said a moment ago that nine out of ten salesmen can learn this technique if they wish. I'll go a long step further: I'll say that I know from actual experience that nine out of ten can also easily learn to use Bill Blake's "hat trick" and Salesman Smith's "close for an opener."

How About You?

Yes, it takes a little practice. It takes a little patience. Above all, it takes an open mind, for the salesman who in his own imagination is already "perfect" will simply go on doing things in his own way, unable to profit from even the best of new ideas.

But for you who are big enough to learn, there's more about closing in Chapter 4 of this book.

SELF-OPERATING QUIZ

Do You Really Act on the Following Facts?

1. That you can't be a strong salesman unless you're a strong closer?............ Yes____ No____

2. That the salesman who *almost* made the sale but didn't get the order is no better off than the man who made the poorest try at that prospect?.................. Yes____ No____

3. That only star salesmen don't need this advice: "You don't close *early* enough; you don't keep on closing *long* enough; you don't try *enough* trial closes between your first and your last"?.............. Yes____ No____

4. That in cases where you don't get a chance to open, you should "go into a close!"? .... Yes____ No____

5. That the myth of the "one psychological moment" for closing has been thoroughly discredited? .... Yes____ No____

6. That "one-blow" closing strategy is always the mark of a very weak closer?.... Yes____ No____

7. That your prospect expects you to carry on (even though he may hope you won't) after he has said "no" to your first few trial closes? .... Yes____ No____

8. That in order to carry on, you've got to be prepared that he may say "no," and be ready to go on with your story?......... Yes____ No____

9. That one big advantage of making multiple trial closes is that if Mr. Prospect says "yes," you win; if he says "no," he very likely gives you some inkling as to why he is holding out?..................... Yes____ No____

10. That it takes an open mind, some practice, and some patience to learn how to use modern closing techniques?......... Yes____ No____

Your score is _____

If you answered "yes" to only seven (or less) of the ten questions, you need a plan to improve your performance. Think it out and write it out *now*, while you've got it in mind!

4

BUYERS LIKE
STRONG CLOSERS

A Smart Idea

You remember Bill Blake—that powerful "closer" I told you about in the previous chapter?

Well, Bill had one idea that I consider so important that I shall give it to you in his own words: "You can always tell a strong closer by what he says in the first sentence of the interview."

Now Bill wasn't talking about the importance of making a good impression right at the start; his idea was that closing technique really begins (or should begin) with your opening remarks.

It's Good Closing or Bad Selling

I mention this because in this chapter I am going to ask you to join me in examining what is probably the most fundamental of all the "facts of life" in salesmanship: the fact that everything the salesman says during an interview is either good closing, or it's bad selling.

Let's start with a run of the mill example. Salesman Jones, who sells for a carpet manufacturer, has just learned that the Hotel Ritz-Plaza is considering the recarpeting of several floors.

"Wow! What a prospect!" says Jones to himself, as he hot-foots it for the hotel.

How to Cool a Hot Prospect

But Jones isn't a heavy closer, so what do you think he does? He opens up something like this: "Mr. Prospect, I'm Jones, representing the Apex Carpet Company. I just happened to be in the neighborhood, so I thought I'd drop in."

Get it? Jones is one of the clan that, for some reason that I've never been able to fathom, figures that the hotter the prospect, the more casual he, the salesman, must appear.

There's a Better Way

A really good salesman would do the opposite. He'd say something like this:

"Mr. Prospect, I'm Brown, representing the Apex Carpet Company. *I'm calling on you today because we are in a position at this time to make a very attractive bid for any carpet you may need.*"

Now unless Mr. Prospect is a very unusual person, his response to Brown's opening will be tenfold as "hot" as his reaction to Smith's. Sure, he's interested in carpets at the moment, but he probably has already half decided where he can get a good buy.

To whom is he more likely to listen: to a carpet man who

just dropped in, or one who has a real reason for calling at this time? One who begins by sparring, or one who opens by making a strong bid for his order?

Selling Is Closing

No, you can't get away from it: Selling is closing, all the way. You walk into a department store. You might buy a new briefcase if you see one you like at the right price.

"Briefcase? What color, sir?" asks the salesgirl. You look, and decide to shop further.

"Briefcase? Let me show you this one. It will hold everything you've got in your old one there, but because of this new feature, it will also . . ."

Well, unless you're a most unusual prospect, the chances of your going back to the first store for that purchase are slim indeed.

But I don't want to give you the impression that I'm talking primarily about first sentences. The same principle holds true throughout the entire interview.

A Dud Steals the Show

For example, I'll never forget a conversation I had some years ago with a travelling salesman who happened to share my table in a dining car, destination Dallas. I don't think I ever learned his name, but I'll always remember him.

We began talking about the weather, I guess, and other in-consequential things, and finally he mentioned that he was hoping that a certain important sample would be waiting for him on his arrival at his hotel.

"It's a dud, but I can't sell without it," he remarked.

I urged him to explain.

"Well, nobody really likes that number," he continued, "and I had just about decided to return the sample, when I found there was a new buyer at a store I sell to. I showed him the line, but it was obvious that he was so new that he was all confused, and wasn't going to buy.

"Suddenly I had an idea. I reached over and picked up the 'dud,' and said, 'Mr. White, this number isn't so hot, so I suggest you don't buy it. Here's another I'd go easy on. But *here* are some items that you can't possibly go wrong on—they're safe.'

"White seemed to realize that I was giving him a straight steer, and we wrote up a pretty nice order."

Sure, It Works

"Well, I kept thinking about the peculiar way I'd gotten that order, and on my next call, I did about the same thing, 'I'm going to show you number 603, but I suggest you pass it up. Here's another item I think you can do without.'

"And when I'd finished showing all my samples, it was the

easiest thing in the world to say, 'Here's the best seller in the line. How about six gross?'

"Believe it or not, it works like a charm. So when I broke number 603 a few days ago, I wired for a replacement, and I'm not making another call until I get it, because I've been selling so much *less* without it!"

You Get the Idea!

You get the idea, of course. The smart carpet salesman starts right in by announcing that he's in a strong position to close. The smart salesgirl holds forth a good reason to buy. The smart wholesale salesman doesn't merely show you his line; he doesn't merely tell you it's a "hot" line; he points out which numbers he *wouldn't* buy, thereby strongly implying that there are other numbers he suggests you *do* buy.

They do these things not to arouse interest, not to create desire, but so that you will be aware during the entire interview that the upshot of it all will be an attempt to *close the sale*.

Think, Act, Plan

Now this principle is closely related to something I know you've heard about before. You've been advised to have confidence, to "think lucky." And maybe you've doubted whether anything as simple as that could possibly increase your selling power.

Well, as I see it, here's how it works. Brown, the strong carpet salesman I mentioned before, may well have started in by thinking he had a good chance to make a sale; but he took another step: He promptly let the prospect in on his secret. And in doing so he took the third and final step in the "lucky" process. His opening remarks showed that he not only "thought lucky," and "talked lucky," but had also "planned lucky."

For you can be sure that Brown, and the girl selling briefcases, and the salesman who pointed out what not to buy, all planned their remarks with care. They are all strong closers because they act on the principle that everything the salesman says during the interview is either good closing or bad selling.

Buyers Go for It

And have you ever stopped to realize how much prospects and buyers *appreciate* this type of selling? Too many salesmen are completely unaware of this important point. And yet what is more natural—more inevitable, in fact—than that a skillful, organized presentation that leads to a "meeting of the minds" should be substantially more agreeable to the buyer than one that "runs around in circles" and therefore ends in lack of agreement! Or, for that matter, even if the result is a sale, what buyer likes to do business with a salesman who expects him to do the salesman's thinking as well as his own?

A Story to Remember

Because realization of this point has been the "making" of more than one star salesman, I'd like to illustrate it with a story that I hope you will remember. It was told to me some years ago by a friend of mine (I'll call him Bob Tyler) who owns a thriving department store in a busy little town in upstate New York.

"Funny thing," said Tyler as we were chatting one day, "how

two salesmen selling the same line can go about it so differently!"

"What's up, Bob?" I encouraged, knowing from past experience that he was leading up to something worthwhile.

Buyers Size Up Salesmen, Too!

"Well," he continued, "for five years now we've been selling the Jim Dandy line of men's shirts." (That isn't the brand name, of course.)

"Yes?" I prodded.

"Couldn't do without them," he reflected.

Then he explained that he had originally tried out the line because a persuasive young salesman had given him a sales talk that "made sense."

"This young chap took care of us for a couple of years, and I was tickled pink when he was made assistant sales manager.

"I greeted his successor with open arms, because by this time we were doing a real job with those shirts. But the new man talked in circles. Oh, lots of salesmen do! Well-meaning and all that, but never had things really thought out."

Tyler paused to relight his pipe. "Three years have gone by, at least, since that change took place. We still sell the line, but not as big as we should and could.

"But here's the point of my story. Every so often this first man—he's now general sales manager—stops off with his salesman for a visit. He still talks sense—makes it easy for us to see why and how we should feature Jim Dandys.

"But between those visits—well, it's tough to buy from a salesman who doesn't know how to tell his own story and how to sell his own goods!"

There you have it in a nutshell. As long as there are buyers and salesmen, there will be salesmen who are "tough" to buy from just as there are buyers who are "tough" to sell to.

Yes, buyers *like* salesmen who know how to sell!

Self-operating Quiz

Do You Really Act on the Following Facts?

1. That you can always tell a strong closer by what he says in the first sentence of the interview? .... Yes___ No___

2. That closing technique begins with your opening remarks? .... Yes___ No___

3. That all salesmanship is either good closing or bad selling? .... Yes___ No___

4. That a casual opening ("I happened to be in the neighborhood, so I thought I'd drop in.") is therefore poor selling?.... Yes___ No___

5. That it also follows that your opening statement should indicate that you intend to make a strong bid for the order—today? .... Yes___ No___

6. That telling a prospect what *not* to buy is often good closing strategy?......... Yes___ No___

7. That buyers actually *appreciate* good salesmanship, because weak selling, which doesn't result in "a meeting of the minds," merely wastes their time?...... Yes___ No___

8. That buyers "size up" salesmen, and are inclined to welcome the man who does an effective job of telling his story?..... Yes___ No___

9. That a salesman who fails to tell an effective story is *tough to buy from?*..... Yes___ No___

10. That it's good selling to keep your prospect aware, during the entire interview, that you are there to get the order?.... Yes___ No___

Your score is _____

If you answered "yes" to only seven (or less) of the ten questions, you need a plan to improve your performance. Think it out and write it out *now*, while you've got it in mind!

5

SIX ELEMENTS OF
SUCCESSFUL SALESMANSHIP

Six Elements of Salesmanship

Have you ever stopped to realize that there's more to salesmanship than selling? As a matter of fact, there are six elements to salesmanship, and selling is but one of them.

You can readily verify this from your own experience as a salesman. You spend only a portion of your working time actually talking to prospects and buyers. That represents the actual selling part of your job.

You Can't Duck It

But you as a salesman also perform many necessary non-selling functions. For example, you travel from prospect to prospect (regardless of whether the distance is a few blocks or many miles); you study the features of your new products; you plan your work so as to waste as little time as possible.

It is probably natural that of these six elements or functions, which I shall list in a moment, the one that we are normally most keenly aware of is the proper use of selling technique, because it is while you are actually talking with your prospect that you are "in the limelight." It is then that the spectacular things are done.

Watch the Other Five

But we cannot afford to let that fact obscure for us the existence and the importance of the other five essentials of salesmanship.

Their significance lies in the fact that when a salesman measures up on all six of these points, you can depend upon it that he is a successful salesman; conversely, where a man is doing only a mediocre job, you can be certain that it is because of a deficiency of one (or more) of the six fundamentals. For this reason alone they merit the attention of each of us who earn our living as salesmen.

What You Sell

1. The first element of salesmanship is knowledge of your product, and the products of your competitors.

Too often this point is confused with the possession of a mere mass of technical information. In actual practice, it may be just as important to know that the Smith Company has used your product exclusively for 20 years as to know that your goods are all wool and a yard wide.

Here's a Test

Here is an interesting and thoroughly practical test of the adequacy of any salesman's product knowledge. It should enable him to do a good job of these things:

(a) Give the information necessary to enable his prospect to buy intelligently.

(b) Give the information necessary to enable his prospect to use, or resell, the product properly.

(c) Answer further questions about the product, should they arise.

(d) Refute ill-founded claims as to competitive disadvantages.

(e) Have a reserve of additional "sales points" for those prospects who are unusually difficult to sell.

(f) Build a sales story so full of fact, persuasion, and enthusiasm that prospects frequently compliment him on his able presentation of his case.

You Can't Win Without It

Any salesman who cannot pass this test with flying colors is falling down on the job. He's off the beam on Element No. 1, and he can't win while that holds true.

Any product, whether a month or a century old, has valid sales points that lend themselves to such treatment. If this were not true, the product would be simply unsalable.

It's part of the salesman's job to dig out, if necessary, the raw materials from which this knowledge can be refined.

Where You Sell

2. The second element of salesmanship is to work your territory (or prospect list) intelligently and adequately.

The best of salesmen pass up more good prospects than they call on. Men of lesser ability score even lower on this point. That's why it is always true that "The better the salesman, the smaller the territory he needs to do a good job." For a top-flight salesman sees many a prospect where an average salesman simply finds deadwood.

It's an Art

Adding new names to your prospect list is an art in itself. So is creating new prospects or markets. So is building an effective follow-up system that compels you to call back on the prospect you have already warmed up, at just the right time to reap the rewards of your earlier effort.

These are but a few of the things involved in Element No. 2.

Few salesmen are able and willing to do a really good job on this score. Here too, there is a simple, practical test to tell you where you stand: Do you always have more "good" prospects to call on than you have time to see?

Why Plan?

3. The third element of salesmanship is a proper planning of work.

I'm not going to take any time to explain how important this is for success in salesmanship. But perhaps you will find the following suggestions helpful:

The sole function of your planning is to enable you:

(a) To go to the right place at the right time.
(b) To avoid waste of time by "doubling back."
(c) To make as many effective calls as you can each day.

Plan or Pay

There's a man I've known for years, who has more sales ability than any ten men you're likely to run into. But he's never been able to learn this simple lesson. As a result, he's paid the price of being just "another salesman" for more than 20 years.

For example, he'll spend precious hours "warming up" prospects or starting new accounts, only to forget to follow them up at the right time. He'll rush the job of planning his next day's calls, with the result that he wastes other valuable hours just getting around. He'll go off on a tangent at the first opportunity and thus leave for tomorrow most of the calls he had planned to make today.

He Gets All the Breaks!

Admittedly this is an extreme example, but it does emphasize the price that must be paid for failing to "Plan your work and work your plan."

Contrast this performance with the motions gone through in the course of the day by a man who has mastered Element No. 3! Too often we hear "He gets all the breaks" or "What a grand territory!" when the correct answer is to be found in the careful planning that alone can produce a day's rounds in which there is a minimum of lost motion.

Strictly Personal

4. The fourth element of salesmanship is that the salesman must personally live up to the name of salesman. For example, he avoids conspicuous errors in grooming and grammar. His

manner is pleasant rather than "grouchy." He avoids the thousand-and-one mannerisms that irritate and distract from what he is saying. His voice is neither a shout nor a whisper. He keeps his appointments. He is "salesminded," and gets a thrill out of selling. He keeps himself in physical condition to work effectively.

These are but random examples of the host of purely personal habits and qualifications that, added together, compose the fourth element of salesmanship.

It is true that these things alone do not make a salesman. It is equally true that every salesman must possess them. You do not need to look far among your own acquaintances to find a man who has everything it takes except some of these personal niceties. He's a second-rate salesman; he lacks one of the six essentials of his craft.

Winners Must Work

5. Element No. 5 is concerned with hard work. It takes hard work to make up and keep up-to-date the product information so essential to success. Endless hard work—for there is an endless flux and change in your products, their application and marketability, your competitors' products, prices, and practices.

It takes hard work to cover your territory intelligently and adequately. It takes hard work to plan your work properly and to work your plan consistently. It takes hard work to achieve and maintain the finest group of personal qualifications of which you are capable.

There are two comments I'd like to pass along on this matter of hard work.

Don't Let It Fool You!

First, the chances are a thousand to one that the fellow who's on top got there by working harder than you'd ever imagine. It's human nature for the leader to try to give the impression that his success is due to skill rather than to hard work. But don't let that fool you.

Secondly, hard work, like almost everything else, is a habit. Maybe you honestly feel today that the fellow who's working harder than you are is missing most of the fun in life.

Very likely that is not the case at all. Chances are that if any man gives "hard work" a fair trial (even that isn't easy for most of us!), he'll soon find that it's fun to be a winner. I've seen many a man who scoffed at success and its attendant efforts change his tune simply because, for one reason or another, he honestly did his best for a while.

Salesmanship Includes Selling

6. The sixth and last element of salesmanship is selling.

Selling technique (discussed in various other chapters in this book) is nothing more or less than doing and saying the right things *while you are in front of your prospect*. It is an art in itself, and the one to which you have probably paid more attention than any other.

But I hardly need point out how much more easily and fruitfully you will be able to apply your selling technique as a result of paying proper attention to the five *other* elements of salesmanship. The man who honestly faces the problems of product information, territory, plan of work, personal qualifications, and industry is not likely to fall down on selling.

Do You Really Act on the Following Facts?

1. That there is more to salesmanship than selling? .... Yes_____ No_____

2. That whenever a salesman measures up on all six elements of successful salesmanship, you can be sure he is doing a top-flight job? .... Yes_____ No_____

3. That whenever a salesman is doing only a mediocre job, you can be sure it's because of a deficiency of one or more of these six fundamentals?.............. Yes_____ No_____

4. That these six elements are concerned with: what you sell, where you sell, how you plan, how you measure up on personal qualities, how hard you work, and how good your selling technique is?.... Yes_____ No_____

5. That it follows from question 4 that *selling* is only one of the six parts of salesmanship? .... Yes_____ No_____

6. That there is a sound, practical six-point test of the adequacy of your product knowledge? .... Yes_____ No_____

7. That there is a sound, practical three-point test of the effectiveness of your planning? .... Yes_____ No_____

8. That any *product,* whether a month or a century old, has valid sales points that can be used to build a sales story so full of fact, persuasion, and enthusiasm that prospects frequently compliment the salesman on his able presentation of his case? .... Yes_____ No_____

9. That it's part of a salesman's job to dig out, if necessary, the raw materials from which this knowledge can be refined?.. Yes_____ No_____

10. That the *best* of salesmen pass up more good prospects than they call on?...... Yes_____ No_____

Your score is _____

If you answered "yes" to only seven (or less) of the ten questions, you need a plan to improve your performance. Think it out and write it out *now,* while you've got it in mind!

6

WHAT MAKES
BUYERS BUY?

There's Always a Motive

Several years ago I happened to see a master salesman close a "million-dollar deal" by skillfully applying this principle: *Behind every sale there is a buying motive.*

I'd like to tell you the story, because exactly the same prin-

ciple is involved in all selling. Whenever the cash register rings in a department store—whenever someone buys a hat, or an automobile, or a rare old work of art—it is because somewhere and somehow that buyer has found an article that he or she has decided will satisfy a certain, specific desire. Curiously enough, that desire is never to own the thing itself, but always rests on something the buyer expects the article will do for him.

Tom Brown Has a Prospect

But to get back to my story, which illustrates this very important point. I was having lunch with a friend—the master salesman I mentioned, who is one of the country's outstanding life insurance salesmen.

As we sat down at our table, he said to me, "See that man over there, at the table by the window? Well, he's a big movie producer, worth quite a few million, and I've got an appointment with him later today to sell him a whopper of a policy!"

"Sounds like a big deal, Tom," I replied. "Think you'll close it?"

"Well, I expect to," was his reply. "He's considering two plans for setting up an estate—mine, which is, of course, based on life insurance, and one suggested by his attorney, which would put his money mostly into other types of investments."

The Prospect Decides

It was only a few minutes later that "Mr. Prospect," on his way out, noticed my friend and stopped at our table.

"Hello, Brown," he greeted him. "Glad to run into you like this, so I can save you a trip to my office. I like your plan, old man, and my lawyer has suggested a good one too, but I've decided to let things rest as they are. No real reason to go ahead with such a plan, for the present at least."

Brown Supplies the Motive

Knowing what was at stake, I held my breath while waiting to see how Tom Brown would react.

"I'm sorry to hear that, Mr. Prospect," he said in a quiet, even tone, "because, since the last time we talked, I've learned that if you adopt my suggestion, you'll become a member of a very exclusive group that any man would be proud to belong to!"

"What group is that?"

"Well, it's a group of less than 150 men, Mr. Prospect, and included are such men as . . ." Here Brown told off the names of half a dozen of America's most successful and wealthiest men. "You see, Mr. Prospect, there are less than 150 men in the whole country who carry the amount of insurance you and I have been discussing. Naturally, it's a very exclusive 'club,' you might say, and . . ."

People Don't Buy *Things*

Brown made his sale before the conversation ended. He made it because he had successfully appealed to what was a strong buying motive in that particular case—the desire to *win the admiration of others.*

Here was something that "leaving things as they were" couldn't offer Mr. Prospect. Since that "something" happened to satisfy a genuine desire on his part, the result was a sale.

It Happens to You

It happens all the time. You decide to buy a new hat. Why? Maybe it's turned spring, and your winter hat is too heavy. In that case, your buying motive is to satisfy a desire for comfort.

Comfort or Vanity?

Maybe, instead, it's because you're a bit ashamed of the looks of your old "fedora." Well, in that event your buying motive is to satisfy your vanity—your desire to look well groomed.

Maybe It's Money Gain

On the other hand, your reason may be that you feel it is "good business" for you, as a salesman, to be well dressed. If so, your buying motive is money gain.

The Salesman Must Help

Now you, as the buyer, may not trouble to think it out that way. You may take a mental shortcut, telling yourself you want a new hat for its own sake. But if the man in the hat store who waits on you is smart, he will realize that his success in making the sale depends on his ability to appeal to your particular buying motive.

Suppose, in your case, it's to gain comfort. He can show you a hundred new hats, rave about their appearance and shout about their low price, but if they are all as heavy as your old winter hat, it's dollars to doughnuts there's no sale.

But let him show you just one hat that promises to satisfy your particular buying motive, and you'll do business even if the price is a bit more than you had expected and the color a few shades removed from what you'd really prefer.

It Applies to All Selling

Now maybe you're thinking, "Well, I can see how all of this is very important to those selling direct to the ultimate consumer, but I sell to people who distribute or resell my products. Their only possible 'buying motive' is to turn over the merchandise at a profit! So all this really doesn't concern me."

But it does concern you! Let me cite you at random several examples of how it does. They will show you that, contrary to what many men in your line believe, the merchant often responds to some buying motive or other that is as strong as, if not stronger than, his desire for simply the maximum "money gain."

Desire for Respect

A man who runs a very successful chain of ladies' ready-to-wear shops once told me, "I buy 'brand merchandise' whenever I can. Oh, I could make just about as much profit selling unknown lines, but when I first started in business, the salesmen selling 'brand names' didn't bother to call on me. I get a 'kick' out of buying from the 'big shots' now that I'm well established and have all those boys calling on me *first*."

As I said, he's very successful. Sure, his main buying motive is to make money. But since he's found he can make money by selling either type of merchandise, he can indulge his preference.

So, if you're calling on him and are selling a "brand line," isn't it smart to appeal to this man's pride—his desire to sell more "brand names" than any of his competitors?

Desire for Security

I know a man who runs a very profitable business as a distributor of industrial equipment. He told me, "I've found that there are often headaches and big losses, as well as big profits, when you buy from manufacturers who aren't amply financed.

Tough adjustments to be made with your customers, too. I sleep better nights if I confine my buying to sources that are well-rated and responsible."

Sure, he's in business to make money. But his buying motive, in the last analysis, is to gain security, rather than maximum profits, and if you're smart you'll appeal to this when you try to sell him.

Pride Is Important

Finally, I know a man who is tremendously proud of his reputation for progressiveness as a manufacturer. Show him a new idea, method, or device that has any valid application in his plant or office, and point out to him that he'll be the first in his city or his industry to adopt it, and you've made a strong appeal to his particular buying motive.

Most Important of All

I've saved for last the most important reason of all why all salesmen, whether selling direct to the consumer or selling for resale, have an equal and common interest in this matter of buying motives.

The point was dramatically illustrated a short while ago in connection with the marketing of a new hydraulic automobile bumper jack. This product had three features, or sales points: ease of operation, adaptability to varying road conditions, and extra safety, as compared with competitive products. Because of these features it bore a higher production cost and selling price than others.

No Sales, No Reorders

The manufacturer's salesmen found wholesalers readily receptive; the wholesalers in turn sold the product to their dealer accounts, but the dealers failed to resell to the public.

A field survey revealed two very interesting facts. First, the dealers were trying to sell on the basis of convenience and adaptability, the two obvious features, but often failed to mention safety, which had not been properly brought to *their* attention. Second, they were encountering price resistance that they couldn't overcome.

But it was also found that if the dealer was asked to emphasize the safety feature, the new product sold easily against its lower-priced competitors!

Learning the Hard Way

Some months of working for nothing could have been spared this manufacturer and his salesmen if the latter had been aware of the principle of buying motives. They would then have done at the beginning what they finally had to do at great cost to themselves. They would have pointed out to the wholesalers the appeal on which their product could and should be sold to the great majority of consumers; the wholesalers' salesmen would have passed this information along to their dealers, and everyone concerned would have shown profits instead of losses, right from the start.

It's Part of All Selling

Yes, you, as a salesman, are definitely concerned with buying motives. You will have taken a long step forward in mastering your art when you have come to the realization that from the *buyer's* viewpoint what you have to offer is never an article, service or product as such, but something that promises to satisfy a desire for comfort, or safety, or wealth, or health; for self-improvement or security of self or dependents; for admiration of others or gratification of some appetite.

These are the things that make the cash register ring, and get the names on the dotted line. A completed sale is nothing more or less than a successful appeal to the particular motive that will make your prospect buy, and simple money gain or pure utility are the answer less frequently than many salesmen realize.

Self-operating Quiz

Do You Really Act on the Following Facts?

1. That there is absolutely no exception to the rule that behind every sale there is a buying motive? .... Yes_____ No_____

2. That the buying motive is never simply to *own* the product or service itself?.... Yes_____ No_____

3. That you yourself have a specific buying motive *whenever* you purchase *anything*? .... Yes_____ No_____

4. That even merchants who buy for resale often have buying motives apart from desire to make a profit?.......... Yes_____ No_____

5. That most buyers are not really aware of what their particular buying motive is? .... Yes_____ No_____

6. That if you succeed in appealing to the correct buying motive, price and other forms of resistance are usually easy to overcome? .... Yes_____ No_____

7. That even if you do not sell direct to the consumer, you should carefully study buying motives, so that you can tell your customers how to resell your product successfully? .... Yes_____ No_____

8. That sales features of your product that seem important to you may leave your prospect "cold," but that he may "warm up" and buy if you present the one that does appeal to his particular buying motive? .... Yes_____ No_____

9. That the key to selling an insurance policy may be pride; a hat, money gain; merchandise for resale, security?....... Yes_____ No_____

10. That the skilled use of buying motives is one of the most important tools in salesmanship? .... Yes_____ No_____

Your score is _____

If you answered "yes" to only seven (or less) of the ten questions, you need a plan to improve your performance. Think it out and write it out *now*, while you've got it in mind!

7

FIVE ROUTES
TO THE TOP

How It All Began

Not long ago a salesman who was really on his toes "sold me a bill of goods."

His technique was so sound, such a fine example of an important principle of modern salesmanship, that I'd like to tell you the story.

I happened to be in a midwestern city of about 100 thousand population, and had almost an hour to wait for the Chicago express. So I walked up the street near the railroad station, looking for a place to get a shoe shine.

As I climbed a chair in "Tony's Shoe Shine, Repair, and Hat Cleaning Parlor," Tony remarked that it was a nice day. I agreed.

Tony Makes a Sale

Then, after a minute of industrious polishing, he stopped and said, "Boss, you needa da new shoe string!"

I looked, and sure enough, Tony was pointing to the evidence. My shoe laces were beginning to show wear.

"Okay," I replied, glad that this suggestion might save me from coping with a broken lace at some unexpected moment.

Tony's next remark was a classic. "Boss, you needa da new heels!"

This time I didn't need to look. I had already noticed signs of wear at the heel, and had decided to do something about it in Chicago. But I looked at my watch and, with a little reassurance from Tony, decided that this was an opportune time to take care of the matter.

Simple Arithmetic

"Nice selling," I mused, taking a good look at this man who in a scant dozen words had more than quadrupled the amount he would ring up on his cash register. How often a day, I wondered, was he able to do it?

With a little encouragement Tony gave me this much information: If he depended on shines alone, plus laces, heels, and hat cleaning that *customers requested*, he could just about support himself. He credited his income from services that *he* suggested as amounting to enough money to support a wife and five small children!

It's the Principle That Counts

Now you and I may employ a more formal arithmetic when we contemplate matters of dollars and cents. We may, in discussing our problems and opportunities, use a brand of English that is far superior to Tony's best.

But, try as we may, we will never achieve a more eloquent statement of one of the principles that distinguish the master salesman from the herd.

FIVE ROUTES TO THE TOP

For there are, after all, only five ways in which you can possibly hope to make today's sales greater than yesterday's. No matter what you sell or where, whether at retail or at wholesale, you are subject, day in and day out, to the immutable principle that increased sales can be achieved only by the following five routes:

Route No. 1

Selling a greater percentage of the prospects you call on or wait on. This is the route of *better closing technique.*

Route No. 2

Calling on or waiting on more prospects. This is the route of *better planning* or *industry.*

Route No. 3

Selling a larger quantity of your product to the prospects you do sell. (Two pairs instead of one, for example; or two carloads instead of one.) This is the route of *better intensive selling*.

Route No. 4

Selling higher-priced merchandise. (A $10 hat instead of one for $6, for instance.) This is the route of *better selective selling*.

Route No. 5

Selling *more* items to the same prospect. (A tie to go with that shirt; or a more complete representation of your whole line, if you sell at wholesale.) This is the route of *better extensive selling*.

There's Magic in Ideas!

Now it happens that Tony's story illustrates Route No. 5. But I've told you the story because it has been my observation that even salesmen who rate near the top on *closing technique* and *planning* or *industry*, rarely even perceive the opportunities that await them if they would but polish up their ideas on intensive, selective, and extensive selling.

Take Andy Burke, for example, who sells a line of furniture to department stores in New England. Well, it took a prolonged illness that ate up Andy's savings and put him in debt to open his eyes.

Andy Goes to Bat

Andy was industrious and a good closer. Nine men out of ten would have decided that he was doing all he could to work his territory effectively. But not Andy! Faced with the need for larger earnings, he hit upon a plan.

"Mr. Jones," he said, as he made his first call after leaving the hospital, "I think your order this spring should be about 50 per cent greater than last year's."

"What?" exclaimed the buyer. "Come now, Burke, you don't mean that, do you?"

Andy Hits a Homer

"Indeed I do," smiled Andy, "because, you see, I've got a plan that will help you sell at least that much more!"

His plan was simple. He had provided himself with some literature from the home office to help the salesmen in the department do a better job of explaining his products.

"Will you see that your salespeople on the floor really read this?" was his first suggestion.

The Record Speaks

Next, he inquired how often in the preceding 12 months his merchandise had been displayed in the store's windows.

"Oh, I guess about four times," was the reply, "but I'll look at the records to be sure."

Well, the records said "once."

Furthermore, had this store used the mats that his firm supplied them free to dress up their newspaper advertising of their products? And the envelope stuffers, and the display materials—had the store even bothered to request them when the home office had offered them *free?*

In short, Andy took an extra half hour to point out some things that store could, and should, do to "pep up" the sale of his wares.

You Know the Answer

You can easily guess the rest of the story. Day by day Andy "polished up" on his plan, adding more and better suggestions as he discussed merchandising methods with various men.

Yes, Andy's increase topped 50 per cent for the next 12 months. Soon it went even higher as buyers and managers came to realize that Andy had become a sort of specialist in helping them increase *their* sales. Continued mention of the brand name by salesmen on the floor, in newspaper advertisements, and elsewhere eventually got the buying public asking for his line by name.

Magic Does It

Why *wouldn't* Andy be eastern sales manager today? Hadn't he broken all records in his territory after he came out of the hospital? And now Andy is teaching the other men in his company the magic that lies in *intensive* selling.

Now there's one thing you'll always find if you explore this matter of increasing sales by selling more intensively, extensively, or selectively. You'll find that each instance is based squarely on an *idea*. Don't expect to travel to success by these routes unless you are prepared to pay the price in brain sweat.

A Bread-and-Butter Example

For generations bread was sold unwrapped. Today, your corner grocer may not even remember that! What happened? Why, some smart wax paper salesman . . .

But wait a minute. For generations it was the housewife who had to slice her loaf of bread. Today, very likely the bread you buy comes pre-sliced.

How come? Somebody had an idea!

The Ideas Are Waiting

And if here and there someone was able to think up a better way of merchandising a loaf of bread, who among us can say that there's not a smart idea lurking around for selling *our* products, just waiting to be thought of? A dozen ideas would undoubtedly be nearer the truth!

I hope you realize from what I've told you that good selling ideas need to be *sound,* but are rarely *spectacular.* And that any intelligent buyer or customer is grateful for your help.

Was I annoyed at Tony the bootblack's painless extraction of a dollar and some change? No, I thanked him. Did Andy Burke's customers resent his way of selling them more? Of course not, they *appreciated* it.

You can be assured that part of your reward for any sound selling ideas you may develop will consist of customer appreciation.

Start Right

Now just a few hints as to how to begin.

Suppose you're selling at retail, and you want to learn how to sell the $10 hat to the $6 prospect. Well, you'll never do it by using any word or gesture indicating that the lower priced article isn't good. On the contrary, you've got to make your prospect feel that he, or she, would be *smart* to buy the $6 headpiece, but even *smarter* to buy the better one!

What It Takes

Being able to do this takes practice, tact, knowledge of your product, and understanding of what makes people buy.

So you see that even this simple example bears out what was said before: You've got to earn your success if you're going to use the route of selective selling! You're not going to increase your sales 66⅔ per cent by mere personality, or pressure, or knocking the low-priced line!

It Takes Planning, Not Wishing

Suppose you're selling to retailers or distributors, and decide your line could be more extensively promoted. You'll never succeed by glib talk that leads only to "loading up" your customer with items he's never bought from you before.

Instead, you've got to put yourself in your customer's shoes. Why *should* he use your line more extensively? How can he sell more and make more money by doing so? What good reasons can you give him for trying your plan?

There's a Better Way!

Yes, there's magic in these five routes to successful selling.

But magic is merely the name for what the other fellow sees when someone applies a new idea. You may not see it at the moment, but regardless of what *you* are selling, there is a better way of doing it than *anyone* is using today.

"Wanted—a new selling idea!"

What a challenge to the man or woman who wants to succeed!

Self-operating Quiz

Do You Really Act on the Following Facts?

1. That there are five, and only five, ways that *any* salesman can ever increase his sales? .... Yes_____ No_____

2. That many salesmen who do a top-flight job of closing, planning, and so forth, lose many sales they could make because they don't know of these five routes to more and bigger sales?....... Yes_____ No_____

3. That to use the principles of intensive, extensive, or selective selling, you must *always* base your program squarely on a sound and specific idea?.............. Yes_____ No_____

4. That such ideas have been developed to increase the sale of even such a run-of-the-mill item as a loaf of bread?....... Yes_____ No_____

5. That such ideas are always *sound*, but rarely *spectacular?* .... Yes_____ No_____

6. That any intelligent buyer is *grateful* if you do a good job of showing him how he will profit by buying more from you than he had intended?................ Yes_____ No_____

7. That there's a better way of selling your product than anyone is using today?.... Yes_____ No_____

8. That every salesman should seriously study how he can use *each* of the "Five Routes to The Top" in his own field?... Yes_____ No_____

9. That if it were your responsibility to direct a group of salesmen, practically all your activities would be concerned with helping every man in the group make the most of these "Five Routes to The Top"? .... Yes_____ No_____

10. That as a salesman practically all your constructive effort is in this same area, whether or not you realize it?......... Yes_____ No_____

Your score is _____

If you answered "yes" to only seven (or less) of the ten questions, you need a plan to improve your performance. Think it out and write it out *now*, while you've got it in mind!

8

LET YOUR PRESENTATION GO MODERN

Modern Buying Is Different

The one thing above all others that distinguishes modern salesmanship from that of days gone by is the fundamental change in our attitude toward the sales presentation.

The reason for this is simple. It is based on the fact that modern buying (and therefore modern selling) is conducted under a different set of conditions.

After all, it's not so long ago that a salesman could get by on personality, a stock of new stories and cigars, and an overdose of "the gift of gab." Not too many years back, the average buyer was likely to be an amateur at his craft. His duties included much in addition to buying; he lacked the training given purchasers today; and above all he could be "spellbound" because he didn't have the detailed and up-to-the-minute knowledge of the market that is now brought to buyers by modern advertising and methods of communication.

Modern Buyers Go for Facts

Today's buyer (whether merchant or housewife) must be sold largely by a presentation of facts. Anyone who's ever tried it knows that a skillful presentation of a set of facts is not easily accomplished.

But that isn't all the modern presentation must reckon with. Consider the intense competition for the buyer's dollar, plus the fact that today's buyer is a busy man or woman and you *begin* to see why it is almost hopeless to try to sell with a hastily improvised story.

Your Big Moment

Of course, every salesman knows in a general sort of way how vitally important it is for him to make the most of his "big moment," that precious time allotted him to tell his story.

For that matter, every salesman who has passed the stage of novice has the *ability* to plan and deliver a talk that is smooth, interesting, to-the-point, and persuasive.

Give Your Good Points a Break!

Yet you probably know as well as I do that in actual practice there are few men indeed who really measure up on this score. In 99 cases out of 100, the reason is a very simple one. The salesman is so busy thinking about the "points" he wants to make that he falls down pretty badly in the way he makes them!

Salesman Jones Listens In

Take Salesman Jones, for example. If he were to hear his own story, told in exactly his own words, given by *another* man, he'd instantly spot a dozen places subject to improvement. Repetition of words and ideas; long, rambling sentences that often obscure rather than clarify; colorless phrases where punch is needed; generalities where precise statements would be of telling value.

You Needn't Be a Genius

It's been my observation that the men who avoid these errors aren't possessed of any special eloquence or unusual talent. As I said before, the average man has the *ability* to do as well.

The thing that sets this smaller group apart from the rest is that they have somehow and somewhere learned one very important lesson: In modern selling you either pay the price of "polishing up" your talk, or you pay the price of losing sales in order to indulge your wish for spontaneity!

I often think how fortunate I was because two little incidents combined to drive this home for me at the very start of my selling career.

Les Made an Art of It

The first took place the day I tagged along with Les Hill on a very important call. Les was a powerful salesman who firmly believed that he owed his success to the meticulous care with which he prepared his sales talk. "You can't sell them unless you can tell them," he often remarked. And you'll see in a moment why I say he had made an *art* of conducting an interview!

Well, Les had just about sold the president of a large concern on a pretty big proposition.

"If you can come back at ten o'clock tomorrow morning," the president had said, "I'd like you to present your proposal to a few of our key men. If they agree, we'll close the deal."

On the way over Les had told me exactly what he was going to say, why, and how. After all, I was there to learn.

Five Men to Be Sold

But no sooner had he been introduced and invited to tell his story, than he ran into trouble. For although three of the "key men" listened attentively, the remaining two did not. You could tell that by the expression on their faces. Finally one took some papers out of his pocket and began to whisper to the other.

Now I'll never forget how Les rose to the occasion! He wasn't going to take the chance of missing out because these two men hadn't heard the strong story he had to tell. Not that lad!

Les Went and Did It

The first thing he did was to "kill" half a minute with some generalities. He spoke these in a tone a bit louder than usual. But this only made the two "whisperers" draw closer together.

Then Les went and did it! All at once he changed his own voice to a little more than a whisper—and took a chance. For as he lowered his voice, he launched into the first of his real points.

It worked! Like magic, it seemed to me at least, although Les told me afterwards that he knew from experience and practice that this tactic would almost surely result in his winning the instantaneous and complete attention of every man in the group.

But Here's the Point

But here's the big point of the story! I don't know whether Les had anticipated the possibility of having a couple of half-hearted listeners on his hands. But I do know that if he hadn't immediately swung into a story that was so smooth that it would have been difficult to stop listening, it's dollars to doughnuts he wouldn't have held the attention of these two men who had something else on their minds! Even I, as a novice, recognized that, and I was fascinated to note how complete his success was. Yes, Les Hill was the first *modern* salesman I ever met!

A Beginner Tries His Luck

Just compare this with the second instance, which occurred a few months later!

This time I was making a call on my own, and you may be sure that I was as far off the beam as any beginner when it came to making a good presentation. I well remember it was a warm day late in May.

That Far-Off Look

As I stumbled along in my talk, pausing now and then for comment, good or bad, I noticed an alarming "far-off" look on Mr. Prospect's face.

Then it happened. He nodded, not in approval, but as part of a catnap!

An Important Resolution

Yes, I got an order. For in the agonizing and endless half-minute that elapsed before a beneficent fly disturbed him back to business, I made an important resolution, and proceeded to act on it, then and there.

"Never, never, again," I promised myself, "will I do anything less than my very, utmost best to prepare a talk that will command and *hold* attention!"

100 to 1

Of course, I needn't have been quite so annoyed with myself, for in the intervening years I've learned that for every man who matches Les Hill's performance, there are at least a hundred who often evoke, if not the nod of sleep, at least the "far-off look" that is but one step removed, or a series of objections, which a smooth sales talk would discourage rather than invite. Or a dozen other sure, though often unrecognized signs that "Here are two men who are not progressing toward a meeting of the minds."

Wanted: a Check

Now, as I said before, it's much easier to catch the flaws if you're listening to the story instead of telling it! I have often told the story of Cal Norton's presentation, to illustrate how difficult it is for any man to appraise his own story, unless he deliberately sets up some sort of check on himself.

Cal Norton Does a Job

It was quite by accident that I ever heard about Cal. It came about when Dan Logan, his boss, showed me with some pride a presentation that one of his men had prepared.

"Name's Cal Norton," he observed, "and I'll tell you how this got on paper. We ran a contest a few weeks ago, and Norton's entry won first prize!"

It's a Honey

There was no doubt about it; this talk was a honey!

"And how close do your men come to using this 'as is'?" I inquired.

Dan picked up the telephone with an "I'll show you" look in his eye. "Send in Bill Jenkins," he requested.

"Bill," he began, after we'd been introduced, "you've learned to follow Cal Norton's presentation pretty well, haven't you?"

Pretty Close to Perfect

"Oh, I follow it all right!" was the reply, and it was obvious Bill was sincere. "Not word for word, of course, but pretty close to it!"

"Okay," said Dan. "Now, just pretend I'm a prospect, Bill, and go to work on me."

Here's what happened. In a four-minute talk, Bill used the word "good" exactly 17 times. (This colorless and almost meaningless word didn't appear even once in Cal's presentation.)

He failed to put into really clear words two very important points. (Cal's presentation made these points so clear that anyone but a moron would understand them.)

He forgot completely to mention one rather important point.

He did not go into a "close" until he had finished his story, although Cal's presentation had three splendid trial closes woven into it.

Finally, it took him four long minutes to deliver an inadequate version of a story that, in its suggested form, can be excellently covered in 90 seconds.

It Can't Happen to You?

"It couldn't happen to me," you may be thinking.

Well, there was nothing wrong with Bill, neither with his memory, nor with his ability to express himself as well as most salesmen. It's simply that Bill *thought* he was doing a really good job—*thought*, in fact, that he had really learned Cal's presentation almost word for word!

Common Sense Will Do the Rest

But I'm not discussing the question of how close to verbatim any salesman should stick in learning a prepared talk. My only point is that any salesman with a modicum of sense will realize what to do once he grasps the fundamental fact that most of us don't do nearly as good a job of telling our story as we ourselves believe.

The Exception Proves the Rule

Perhaps it's the exceptions that really prove this point!

Les Hill, for example, was not only given to endless "polishing" of his talk, but even practiced before a mirror. It's surprising how many master salesmen use this and other props to keep themselves informed of what the other fellow sees and hears when he's listening to them!

Practice Makes Perfect

I happen to know a trial attorney who belongs to that clan of wizards who almost always sway judge, jury, and spectators

to their way of thinking. His brilliant persuasiveness seems so completely unrehearsed! Yet it is in reality the product of a gruelling program of planning and polishing and memorizing *before* he enters the courtroom.

Oh, yes, he speaks well when occasion demands that he "rise" unprepared. But he has told me that he rates his own effectiveness at such times at 30 per cent of his regular "stride."

Have You 70 Per Cent to Spare?

Well, a 70 per cent shrinkage in effectiveness means a loss of 70 per cent of the cases, or sales, that could and should have been won! That's a figure to give any man reason to ponder.

Selling Is Telling

You can see why whenever a salesman asks me for the rules or principles that will guide him in building a more effective sales talk, I always reply, "There's only one approach I know of that will do you any real good.

"You've got to begin by becoming so presentation conscious that before you're through polishing your talk, every single word, phrase and idea in it will be the best you can find for the particular job it's got to do.

"You'll know your presentation is ready when you reach the point where, if a prospect lets you state your case, you'll know in advance that the order's practically in the bag!

"No, you can't *sell* them unless you can *tell* them. Modern selling technique begins with modern *telling* technique!"

SELF-OPERATING QUIZ

Do You Really Act on the Following Facts?

1. That modern buying — and therefore modern selling — differs from that of former days? .... Yes____ No____

2. That today most buyers, whether merchant, housewife, purchasing agent, or consumer, are well informed, too busy to waste time, and solicited by many who want the same dollars (or order) that *you* do? .... Yes____ No____

3. That under these circumstances, an opportunity to tell your sales story is "your big moment," one too valuable to be handled with an improvised story or an attempt at old-fashioned, fact-poor "spellbinding"? .... Yes____ No____

4. That every salesman has the ability to plan and deliver a talk that is smooth, interesting, to-the-point, and persuasive? Yes____ No____

5. That most salesmen fail because they are so busy trying to think of the "points" they want to make that they don't give enough thought to *how* they ought to make them?................ Yes____ No____

6. If any salesman were to hear his own sales story, exactly as he himself tells it, he'd probably spot a dozen places where it is subject to improvement?.......... Yes____ No____

7. That "you can't *sell* them unless you can *tell* them," and you can't *tell* them unless you pay the price of really working hard at polishing up your talk?........ Yes____ No____

8. That for every man who does an outstanding job of telling his story, there are at least 100 who fail? .... Yes____ No____

9. That most of us don't do nearly as good a job of making our presentation as we think we do? .... Yes____ No____

10. That a famous trial attorney has stated
    that he rates himself only 30 per cent
    as effective when he talks spontaneously
    as when he has completely prepared?. . Yes_____ No_____
                                   Your score is _____

If you answered "yes" to only seven (or less) of the ten questions, you need a plan to improve your performance. Think it out
and write it out *now*, while you've got it in mind!

9

CAPITALIZE
YOUR PROSPECT'S
OBJECTION!

Meet Ted—A Specialist

Ted Wilson is a smart apple. He's got to be! Ted is also a specialist; and again, he's got to be to hold down his job!

Ted spends practically all of his time answering prospects' objections. It works out that way because Ted's sole job is to call back, with his company's salesmen, on those prospects whom the salesmen have found too "tough" to handle by themselves.

Now there's a job for a man who can take punishment! And dish it right back too! If there's anybody in selling who is more adept than Ted at skillfully handling an objection, I'd certainly like to meet him.

The More Objections the Better

But don't get the idea that Ted engages in either "pressure tactics" or "rough-and-tumble" comebacks. On the contrary, he proceeds on the rather unique idea that an objection is really a very valuable piece of *sales ammunition!*

For example, Mr. Prospect may say, "No, I can't afford the money to put in the equipment you suggest."

And Ted replies, "Mr. Jones, I'm glad you mentioned that, because one of the big features of our equipment is the money it saves you, from the very first minute you install it."

Then he proceeds to prove his point.

That's Capitalizing!

Now you'll agree, I'm sure, that in handling the matter that way, Ted has accomplished much more than merely answering or disposing of an objection. He has actually capitalized it! For he has seized on the key word or thought of the prospect's objection itself, and turned it to his own advantage.

That Suits Me Fine

He has merely put into more salesworthy words this thought: "Okay, Mr. Prospect, so you're money-minded! Well, that suits me fine, because the more you emphasize *your* point, the greater significance and weight you are giving to one of *my* best arguments: Our equipment more than pays for itself in a reasonable time. So, thanks, Mr. Prospect, for telling me what's really important to you, and for giving me a chance to get in a good, telling argument!"

They're All Grist for Ted's Mill

It's surprising how many objections Ted is able to handle in this way.

For example, a certain prospect once objected, "No, Mr. Wilson, I'm not interested in hearing your story. We've been buying our equipment from the Smith Company for almost 20 years. We have confidence in them and their values, and we've learned how to use their product, so it's no use."

Now a lesser man than Ted would have found himself on the defensive. What could you say to that unless you were willing to "knock" a competitor?

Get Your Foot in the Door

But not Ted! He's smart, as I've said. He saw in this objection a grand opportunity to "get his foot in the door!"

"Mr. Prospect," he replied, "you've put your finger right on the big point! We know, of course, that you buy from Smith, and that they're a fine outfit, and that you're accustomed to their product. We know that we'd simply be wasting your time as well as our own if we didn't have something awfully attractive to show you to overcome that big handicap. And if we do, I'm sure the least you want to do about it is hear our story!"

Thanks for the Opportunity

No, Ted wasn't on the defensive. "Mr. Prospect," he was saying in effect, "thanks for setting up the Smith Company as a sort of ideal. For that gives me a chance to give you my whole argument (which is, of course, that even with two strikes against us, we can win out if you'll only make a comparison) right off the bat!"

Let's Take a Tough Example

But I mustn't forget to tell you how Ted's technique applies to an objection that is the bane of many a salesman's life: the price objection! You know how often you, as a salesman, run into that one!

Well, let's take an example that for most men would be a "toughie," the prospect who arbitrarily sets up price as an obstacle, without relating it to actual value.

"No," says Mr. Prospect, "I simply won't pay any such price. Why, I can beat that by 15 per cent!"

Watch Ted Go to Town

Now watch carefully! Does Ted argue the fact, or what's just about as futile, try to justify his price? Not he!

"Mr. Prospect," he says quickly, "it wasn't my impression that your products are the very cheapest in your field. Was I wrong?"

Nine times out of ten that does it. For 90 per cent of the people you call on, whether manufacturers, doctors, merchants, or what-have-you, do not operate on a single "I'm the cheapest in town" appeal.

And, what's equally important, they really know that price

is meaningless when it is considered apart from quality. All Ted does is to tell them in the fewest possible words that he knows they know it!

Six Million Dollars Can't Be Wrong

But for the odd case where more is needed, Ted follows through with this:

"Besides, Mr. Prospect, we do six million dollars a year, all at these same prices. We sell some of the best people in the land. So I think you'll find that our prices are right for what we have to offer."

Nobody Misses by a Mile!

But I purposely picked a tough example, and in such a case Ted might have to go even one step further.

"You say we're 15 per cent above our lowest competition. Well, I can see how we might get away with it if we were 1 per cent or maybe 2 per cent off the beam, but do you honestly think we could stay in business if we were that far off? Do you think we could sell such people as the . . . ?" (Here Ted mentions some names that carry lots of weight in his particular field.)

What's the Score Now?

Now let's see what Ted has accomplished by each of his points. First, he's called Mr. Prospect's bluff that price is all that counts; next he's just about proved that his product's price-value relationship is sound and attractive; finally he's used both tact and deadly logic to blast away an absurd claim.

Just Blow Your Own Horn

But note this carefully, please: *In each one of these steps, Ted has capitalized the prospect's objections.*

For he has done much more than refute. He has skillfully said, or strongly implied, in each of these three steps, some very favorable things about his company or product (or both) that would have remained *unsaid* had the objection itself never been raised.

Wanted: More Objections!

Yes, that's the essence of Ted's technique. That's why he *welcomes* an objection. For his own case is better off than if the objection had not been offered. And you'll see, I hope, why it automatically follows that the more energetically the objection is voiced, the greater the "step forward" that Ted's technique achieves for *his* side of the discussion.

It Works on Complaints, Too

Now I think you have heard enough about this technique to enable you to see its application to *all* selling. For example, probably you, like all of us, occasionally run into a prospect (or even a good customer!) who doesn't approve of some feature of your products, or perhaps some policy or practice your company follows.

You will have to use your own judgment as to how far you ought to go into the merits of the complaint, or, indeed, whether you should consider it at all. But you'll also find it a grand opportunity to *capitalize* the complaint by pointing out the general responsibility of your concern, the widespread and continued acceptance of its products (and related points). Not only will this go far to dispel the objection or complaint by putting it in its proper subordinate position, but it will also leave you in a stronger position than before.

Don't Minimize—Capitalize!

"I don't see why you people have so many different models in your line," a prospect or customer may say. "It means we've got to carry such a large inventory."

The average salesman would probably reply, "We have only eight models in our line, Mr. Prospect, and we really can't get along with less."

Well, that's an attempt to *minimize* the objection. Isn't it a lot smarter to *capitalize* it, using as much of the following as circumstances seem to justify?

Here's How to Do It

"I know how you feel, Mr. Prospect, for as you may know, we serve over a thousand retailers, and that question has come up before. Only recently Mr. Blank of the Blank Company (mention a big name if you can!) brought it up too.

"Well, in our 40 years as manufacturers of this line, we've always tried hard to protect our retail outlets, and I'm sure you'll find that the volume of business you'll get on all eight of our models will more than justify the inventory you'll need."

Now, as I said, you may not want to use all of your "capitalizing" arguments at any given time, but I've yet to meet the salesman who didn't find this an extremely effectual method of handling such a situation, once he had learned Ted's technique.

Here's an Extra Dividend

I hope you have decided to use it too! If you have, there's an invaluable "extra dividend" awaiting you!

It works like this. As soon as a little thought and practice give you the "feel" of this technique, you'll find that in addition to being the top-drawer method of meeting *objections,* it also serves as a tremendously important means of building a powerful presentation.

Here's How It Works

For example, if you're going to call on the Brown Company and have learned that they have been buying exclusively Smith products for 20 years, you will not open your presentation with a description of your own line.

Instead, you'll begin by saying that you know they use Smith products, that the Smith Company is very reliable, and that you wouldn't waste their time or your own by calling unless you had something *attractive enough to overcome that big handicap.*

You've Anticipated the Brushoff

Yes, you use the same words as were cited earlier in this chapter, only this time, you're using them as a strong opener to your presentation. You know the "Smith objection" will be on your prospect's mind, so you decide you might just as well meet it, and what's more, *capitalize* it, to make sure you'll get an attentive hearing.

There's More to Be Said

Because it's always an unremoved objection that's to blame whenever any salesman fails to get his order, I'll give you some additional suggestions on this vital subject in Chapter 10.

SELF-OPERATING QUIZ

Do You Really Act on the Following Facts?

1. That a skillful salesman can actually *capitalize* practically every objection?.. Yes_____ No_____

2. That an objection is usually a valuable piece of ammunition for a competent salesman? .... Yes_____ No_____

3. That it is a sign of weakness to go on the defensive, or simply to try to refute an objection, since the proper way to handle it is to *capitalize* it?............ Yes_____ No_____

4. That this same method works well in handling complaints, too? .... Yes_____ No_____

5. That *minimizing* an objection is only one step better than going on the defensive, since your job is to *capitalize* it?....... Yes_____ No_____

6. That once you get the swing of "capitalizing," you also get, as an extra dividend, a strong *opener* for your presentation, in those cases where you expect a "brush-off"? .... Yes_____ No_____

7. That it's always an unremoved objection that's to blame whenever any salesman fails to get the order? .... Yes_____ No_____

8. That "capitalizing" can be used very effectively against the "price" objection?.. Yes_____ No_____

9. That it can be used very effectively against the "married-to-your-competitor" objection? .... Yes_____ No_____

10. That it can be used very effectively against the "can't-afford-it" objection?.. Yes_____ No_____

Your score is _____

If you answered "yes" to only seven (or less) of the ten questions, you need a plan to improve your performance. Think it out and write it out *now*, while you've got it in mind!

10

OBJECTIONS AREN'T HARD TO HANDLE!

It's All in Knowing How

Any salesman who has learned how to capitalize his prospects' objections has, of course, also learned to welcome them. The more the merrier, for they're all grist for his mill!

But there's more to be said on this important subject, and I'll begin with those objections that a salesman needn't bother to meet at all.

Salesman White, for example, sells California-made sports togs to department stores in the East.

"I don't think we're interested in your line," objects Buyer Black, "since we can buy similar merchandise right in New York City. It's easier and quicker for us all around if we buy lines made in our own back yard."

Well, Let's Ignore It

Here is a "natural" for any salesman who knows how to *capitalize* an objection. But White may decide for very good reasons (such reasons are discussed below) that in this particular case he'd rather *ignore* (or evade) the objection. So ignore it he does!

Of course, he's got to know how. So he simply says, "Mr. Black, I'll tell you in a minute how we handle that problem. But first I'd like to show you how you can get some extra volume by handling our line, selling customers you can't sell in any other way."

Buyers Are Like That

Now it's an unusual prospect who won't respond to that technique. "For after all, if there's really extra business to be had, maybe the problem isn't so important . . . and anyway, hasn't Salesman White said he'd come back to that later?" he reasons with himself.

But curiously, there's probably no need to go back to that subject again. For if White succeeds in convincing his prospect that there are important advantages in selling his line, the logical decision to go ahead won't be reversed by what is, after all, a relatively minor point.

It's a Familiar Pattern

And perhaps you've guessed already why White decided that in this instance it was best to evade, rather than capitalize, his prospect's objection. He did so because he recognized a very familiar pattern: "Buyer expresses objection—really it's relatively unimportant—best way to prove this is to call attention to the things that are important—original objection will simply disappear in the process."

Some Won't Be Ignored

Now I'd like to be sure that you understand clearly when it's good selling to ignore an objection, and when it isn't.

If Buyer Black had said, for example, "I'm not interested in your line because you sell to our competitor across the street," or "I'm too busy to look at any lines this week," obviously it would be the poorest of tactics to attempt to evade the objection. An alert salesman who knows how can easily *capitalize* these and similar obstacles. So capitalize he does!

The Two for You

Now there are other methods of meeting objections besides the two already discussed. But any man who really masters these two will not only find himself admirably equipped to handle 98 per cent of all possible objections, he will also undoubtedly recognize that other methods, even where they do succeed, are almost always slower, and produce a less satisfactory over-all result than the two he has learned to use.

Man Bites Dog

But just as there are objections that should be ignored, there are others that a smart salesman will make certain to bring up himself, even if his prospect does not!

Perhaps you've never stopped to realize it, but this is the technique that master salesmen use *above all others* to make those tough sales that the average salesman simply cannot get to first base on.

There's Always a Reason

Let Roy Mayes, a heavyweight salesman if ever there was one, tell you about it in his own words.

"When I took over the Chicago territory," Roy told me one day, "I asked my predecessor why he had found it almost impossible to break into any of the good retail accounts there.

"He told me that the answer was simply that we were doing much less consumer advertising in that area than one of our competitors, and retailers felt our line would be more difficult to sell."

"Well, that must have been easy for you to handle, Roy," I observed.

The Salesman Objects!

"It was!" he replied with a smile. "I simply made sure that this particular objection was brought right out in the open!

"'Mr. Retailer,' I'd begin, 'I'm sure you've heard of our line, even though you don't sell it. To save your time and mine, I'd like to ask whether our advertising policy has anything to do with that.'

"And when Mr. Retailer said 'yes'—which he always did—I had him! Because I'd take as much time as necessary, right then and there, to prove to him that our long-standing reputation, plus our effective *class* advertising in his locality, meant there was a substantial market for our line, just waiting to be sold!"

"Grand!" I applauded. "But tell me, Roy, did you ever find out why your predecessor didn't do exactly the same thing?"

"You bet I did. I made it a point to ask him." Roy was like that.

"And do you know what he told me? He said that for the first six months he was there, he didn't even know *why* the 'big shots' weren't buying our line!"

"Well, I can understand that," I said, "but how about the next twelve months? He was there a year and a half, wasn't he?"

The Less Said the Better

"Right," said Roy. "And those last twelve months should have been a picnic for him! But he missed the boat completely, I'm afraid, for he told me that when he did find out what the resistance was based on, he decided that the less said about it the better! Belongs to the school of salesmen who never bring up an objection!"

"There's one thing more, Roy," I said. "Do you happen to know whether he knew there was such a good answer to this objection?"

"Sure he knew!" Roy took a piece of paper out of his brief-case. "Here's the whole thing, in a letter from the home office, sent to him when he complained that we'd never sell much in that territory until we spent more money for advertising!

Some Buyers Won't Tell You

"But, as I said, he believes in never *bringing up* an objection. So sometimes it was never even mentioned, even though it was the real reason why that particular buyer wouldn't buy.

"Even when it was brought out, it was perhaps tied in with some other objection, or so late in the interview that there wasn't time to handle it properly."

"And," I took over the story from Roy, "of course, then he was on the defensive, instead of *capitalizing* for all he was worth!"

A Funny Notion

"That's right," said Roy, "and now I wish you'd tell me how any salesman comes by the notion that it's never good selling to raise an objection."

So I told Roy, in a few words, something you probably already know.

"Not every salesman," I said, "has as sound an attitude to-ward objections as you do.

"Some haven't learned that if an objection is in a prospect's mind, and is important enough to him so that it will be a real factor in arriving at a final decision, there's nothing in the world that's more important for the salesman to discuss!"

You Must Know How!

"Yes," Roy agreed, "that's right. Objections aren't hard to handle—unless, of course, you don't know how!"

And that "how" boils down to just four points. You must know how (and when) to capitalize, to ignore, and to raise objections if you're really on your toes. But there's one remaining point that's just as vital as the other three. You must know how to handle a kind of objection that easily qualifies as any salesman's kindest friend!

There's a Friend for You!

This is the type of remark that, although an objection in form, is really a tip-off that the buyer wants you to take out your order pad and close the deal.

You've met it often, I'm sure. You're trying to sell a set of law books to an attorney, let's say. You've told your story, or most of it. "Well, I really should talk it over with my partner, I guess," says your prospect.

If you're a *real* salesman, you instantly feel the thrill of victory, because to you those words have said in unmistakable terms, "I've decided to *buy!*"

The Missing Partner

How do you know it? There are a dozen signs. If Mr. Lawyer were still unsold, he'd choose words that have an entirely different meaning, in spite of their apparent similarity. He'd say, "No, I've got to talk it over with my partner." Undoubtedly his *tone* and *manner* would be different too.

In the first case, they convey to the alert salesman, "Just give me a little reassurance that my partner won't mind."

In the second, the message is, "I'll do nothing about this matter without discussing it with my partner."

You've done the same thing yourself, as a buyer, a thousand times. "I wish you had exactly this same suit in a double-breasted model," you remark to the salesman. He notes your words, your tone, the expression on your face, the fact that you are still clutching the single breaster in your hand.

"Mister, you've bought yourself a suit, single-breasted," is what he tells himself. For he knows that if you hadn't, you would have said instead, "I like this material, but I want a double-breasted coat. Have you got one?"

When "No" Means "Yes"

Again, although the words are basically similar, there is a tremendous difference in the degree of their finality.

In the first version the attorney and you, the prospect for a suit, are both doing the same thing—you are getting an objection out of your system; you're disposing of it yourself!

But in the second version, they are announcing that there is a real objection that, as yet, has not been overcome.

Sure, It Hurts

Now, it's painful to watch any salesman who treats such a "buying signal" as an objection, simply because he can't distinguish between the two. Fortunately, most salesmen don't make that mistake.

But it's almost tragic to see a salesman who, although he recognizes it as a buying signal, is clumsy enough to *treat* it pretty much as he would an objection, nonetheless. That's a very common mistake!

Fragile—Handle With Care!

Yet it's one that is really very easy to avoid. The "secret" is that, from the instant your prospect has "told" you he's made a favorable decision, your sole job is to avoid *disturbing* that favorable outcome.

You may be—you very likely are—right in the middle of a "point." Drop it! Drop it then and there, or you're more than apt to talk yourself out of an order.

Take the attorney who "guesses" he should consult his partner. You pause as he speaks, and forget every single word of additional selling argument you may have in reserve. You say something like this: "Shall we bill this with the cash discount, or would you prefer the four-payment plan?" Or you say any one of a thousand other things—little, noncontroversial things that have this qualification: They won't disturb the sale!

You know what is likely to happen if you reopen a sale that's closed! And of course, that's exactly what you'd be doing if you proceeded either to use *additional* sales talk, or if you went into the "pros and cons" of waiting to talk it over with the missing partner.

Going Up!

So you see, "Objections aren't hard to handle; unless, of course, you don't know how!"

Not that it's easy to know how—it's not like falling off a log, for instance.

But even beginning to learn how is fun. *Mastering* the "big four" rules will take any man to the top. Yes, it will do that, as long as there are goods and services to be sold!

SELF-OPERATING QUIZ

Do You Really Act on the Following Facts?

1. That an important secret of handling objections is to develop skill in detecting those that aren't really important in the buyer's own mind, and then simply *evading them?* .... Yes____ No____

2. That it's very important to make the proper decision as to whether an objection should be met (capitalized) or evaded (ignored)? .... Yes____ No____

3. That if your prospect has an objection *in his mind,* but doesn't mention it, it is part of your job to "get it out in the open," so that you can remove it by the proper method? .... Yes____ No____

4. That it follows from the preceding statement that there is no validity to the old rule, "Never bring up an objection"? ... Yes____ No____

5. That the sound rule is to decide whether that particular objection seems really important to the prospect, and if it is, to bring it out in the open if he doesn't do so himself? .... Yes____ No____

6. That statements that are objections *in form* are sometimes really signals that the prospect is *ready to buy?* .... Yes____ No____

7. That you have gone a long way toward mastering the technique of handling objections effectively when you have learned how to decide when to *capitalize,* when to *evade,* when to *bring up* an objection, and when a so-called objection is really a buying signal? .... Yes____ No____

8. That when the prospect voices a buying signal, you should stop further "sales talk," and with a few words of reassurance ask him to sign the order? .... Yes____ No____

9. That the salesman's treating the buying signal as an objection almost always loses the sale? .... Yes____ No____

10. That the four rules here set forth (Capitalize, Evade, Bring up, Close) cover 99 per cent of the problems connected with objections? .... Yes____ No____

Your score is _____

If you answered "yes" to only seven (or less) of the ten questions, you need a plan to improve your performance. Think it out and write it out *now*, while you've got it in mind!

11

EVERY SALESMAN
HAS TWO BOSSES

Meet Your Bosses

The wisest sales manager I ever knew once said to me,
"Every salesman has two bosses, his sales manager and himself."

The thought behind that simple remark is so utterly important that I say without hesitation to any salesman:
"Whether you have achieved the pinnacle of success, or
whether you have despaired of your ability to sell—here is a
message that you cannot afford to miss!"

Those are strong words, and I would not use them to intro-
duce any other message that I have for you. But I think you'll
find them justified.

For Example . . .

A run-of-the-mill example will illustrate the point. Salesman Jones, in spite of his better than average ability, has been doing a below-average job. His sales manager calls Jones in to talk things over, and after a complete and frank discussion, Jones realizes that the trouble is due to his lack of proper planning. And as the two men part, Jones has made a firm resolve to lick that weak spot—today.

Well, 60 days go by; what has happened? Jones is on top of the list! Now I don't know how you feel about it, but I say that the lion's share of the credit for that achievement belongs to Jones himself. True, he would never have found himself had he been left to himself. But neither his sales manager's analysis of his difficulty, nor his own resolve to correct a bad habit, would have been worth a hoot if *Jones hadn't followed through.*

It's Not Easy

To see this matter in its proper light, we've got to realize that correcting a bad habit is rarely easy.

Yes, you and I may find it easy to plan our work. But it so happens that Jones didn't, and that's precisely the reason he didn't do it from the beginning! You and I can take any bad habit *we've* got (all of us have some, you know) and we can look around us and see dozens of men for whom that particular problem has never existed! Yet that doesn't automatically make it easy for us to follow suit.

Your Part of the Job

No, the more you go into this matter of progress and success, the more you realize that far and away the biggest portion of sales management that any man is subjected to comes directly from himself.

This principle is so obvious that it needs no further illustration. But there's more to be said on where and how to apply it. For, as I remarked before, recognizing the spot that needs repair is one thing; repairing it is another!

So I'm going to give you a few examples, based on my personal experience, of how other men have gone about it.

From the Bottom to the Top

Of course, you know how important *closing* is. Well, Ken Gray, by really good "self-sales-management," transformed himself in a couple of weeks from a very poor closer into a very good one!

Ken's trouble—a common one, by the way—was that he was afraid to make a strong bid for the order. Time and again, when he had a man just about sold, he'd flunk out on some little objection like, "Well, maybe I'd better think it over for a day or two." That was Ken's signal to pack up and leave!

Knowing Isn't Enough

All the coaching I'd given him, both in and out of the field, had apparently gone to waste. Sure, Ken had learned what he should do, but actually doing it was something else again.

But all at once the impossible happened. Ken's sales soared to the point where, knowing his handicap, I almost thought he was carrying a shotgun to help him do the job!

But the explanation was really very simple. "You remember

that little talk we had, about two weeks ago?" he began. "Well, the figures you showed me that day made it very plain that I had gotten exactly nowhere during the past year. Still a weak sister at closing!"

"That's right, Ken," I agreed.

"I got to thinking that maybe the best thing for me to do would be to quit. *That gave me an idea!*"

"Go on," I urged, "I'm all ears!"

Gray continued, " 'Ken,' I said to myself, 'if you knew right this minute that you weren't going to be in your territory more than a week longer, you'd push each man for all he's worth during the next few days, wouldn't you?'

Last Call

"So I made a list of every important prospect I'd developed and decided that I'd make just one final call on each. Whether he bought or not, that was going to be the last time I'd see him.

"Well, on such a call there'd be no need to pull any punches. So when my first prospect tried to brush me off with the old dodge about thinking it over . . ."

Now I think you'll agree that that's a classic example of superb "self-sales-management"! Here was a job that no one under the sun could do for Ken except Ken Gray himself!

Two Things to Note

There are just two things more I'd like to tell you about this victory.

The first is that although Ken's new closing tactics seemed like "high pressure" to *him*, in actual fact they were nothing more than any strong closer uses every day in the week. I made it a point to find out.

The second point is that if I were to tell you Ken's right name, you'd doubtless recognize him as heading up a well-known, hard-hitting sales force. Yes, a lot has happened in the intervening years since that day when Ken just about decided that he couldn't sell!

Marty's a Has-Been

Marty Rogers comes to my mind just about every time I think about presentations. When I first met him, back when the last depression was about five years old, I had quite a surprise.

I had been forewarned that here was a "has-been." Probably walk into my office with the help of a cane, I had decided. For his record showed that he had nose-dived from a "hot potato" pace right down to the bottom end of the list. There he'd stayed for the past four or five years, in spite of every effort to dislodge him. Now it was my turn to go to work on him.

But I was in for a surprise, as I say. In walked Marty, not only under his own power, but with something that looked suspiciously like some extra zip. We hadn't talked for more than two minutes before I realized that here, in spite of the record, was a man who *ought* to be on top.

"Marty," I finally said, "you seem to have things pretty well under control. You plan your work and work your plan. You know your products and aren't afraid of competition. You're a good talker and a strong closer."

A Fair Weather Salesman

"Sure I am," was his reply, "and if my territory hadn't gone to pot a few years ago, if only I had a live prospect to call on now and then, you'd see me head the list again, the way I did for 15 years!"

"Well, before we go into that," I continued, "there's just one thing we haven't covered. I'd like to hear the presentation you use in the field."

Marty snorted eloquently. "I knew we'd come to that!" and he launched into a tirade against the notion that any salesman who had blood and guts should even consider what he would say to a prospect until the interview itself was on. He did such a strong job of it that I knew here was one talk he'd learned to tell well!

"Okay, Marty," I finally managed to interrupt, "I get your point. I believe in prepared presentations, and you don't, so I'll compromise with you!"

Well, that seemed to take Marty by surprise.

"Tell you what we'll do," I continued. "You know Bill Elliot is being made a district manager in about six weeks . . ."

Marty Gets a Break

"Say!" shouted Marty. "That will open up about the best territory . . ."

"Sure," I agreed. "Bill's broken all sorts of records in it. Must be good."

"I'd give my right arm for it, that's what!"

"Well, I think you can have it, if you really *want* it, Marty. But remember we were going to *compromise*. You've got to do something that *I* want, too. You've got to prove in the next six weeks that you're able to learn, and use in the field, our standard presentation."

Poll Parrot Stuff

Marty almost choked at that. But he finally agreed, "If it really will make you happy to see whether I qualify as a poll parrot, I guess I'll have to show you. But you'll let me sell in *Bill's* territory any way I want to, right?"

It Never Fails

Perhaps you've anticipated the result. Marty found he didn't want to move into Bill Elliot's territory, after all. After about a week of valiant struggle with the sales talk that he disliked so heartily, Marty made a startling discovery: There were enough live prospects in his own neck of the woods to keep him plenty busy the rest of his natural life!

Now I've picked this example for a specific reason. You remember what I told you about Salesman Jones and Ken Gray. The problem they had was to make themselves do something in which they already believed. But Marty Rogers' problem was different. There was never any question in his mind, nor anyone else's, that he could master and use a prepared talk if he wanted to. Only, he'd never *wanted* to!

An Area That's All Yours

All three of these examples are alike on the main point. All three show that for each of us who sells there is an area of management that is necessarily an area of personal operations! No sales manager—except yourself—can really lick your bad spots.

You can be shown *how* to perform a certain task; you can see examples of the right way to do it. But in the final analysis, only your own self-discipline and desire to reach the top will determine just how far you will go toward that goal.

By the same token, no one can *stop* you from realizing the fullest success of which you are capable except, again, your old friend, you!

SELF-OPERATING QUIZ

Do You Really Act on the Following Facts?

1. That *you* have "two bosses," your sales manager and yourself? .... Yes_____ No_____

2. That only *you* can see to it that you *follow through* on a sound plan, regardless of whether you or your sales manager *devised* the plan? .... Yes_____ No_____

3. That it follows that a salesman who improves his score deserves the major part of the credit for his performance?...... Yes_____ No_____

4. That correcting a bad habit is rarely easy? .... Yes_____ No_____

5. That we all have some bad selling habits? .... Yes_____ No_____

6. That recognizing a habit that needs correcting is one thing but actually correcting it is another? .... Yes_____ No_____

7. That many of our problems can in fact be overcome *only* by such "self-sales-management"? .... Yes_____ No_____

8. That "self-sales-management" is needed for these two purposes: *to do* the things we *believe* in but haven't mastered, and *to try out* things we *don't* believe in but which are urged upon us by someone else who usually knows what he's talking about? .... Yes_____ No_____

9. That there is no "bad selling habit" that can't be licked with a reasonable amount of determination and patience?........ Yes_____ No_____

10. That one "bad selling habit" can nullify a dozen good ones? .... Yes_____ No_____

Your score is _____

If you answered "yes" to only seven (or less) of the ten questions, you need a plan to improve your performance. Think it out and write it out *now*, while you've got it in mind!

12

PLAY BALL WITH YOUR BIGGEST CUSTOMER

Something New Under the Sun

There is one aspect of the "selling game" that is long overdue for an airing. Although it is an important part of modern salesmanship, all too often it is utterly ignored, even by salesmen who measure up well on all the other points comprehended in the term "salesman."

I am referring to nothing more or less than the importance, yes, the growing importance, of playing your part as a member of an organization, the company you work for.

Don't Miss a Good Bet

Now I am sorry for any salesman who lacks either the time or the inclination to think this thing through. He's deliberately missing a good bet. How good a bet, we'll see in the next few minutes.

Eddie Skinner Is a Card

Eddie Skinner is quite a card. Nobody takes him very seriously—nobody, that is, in the home office. Eddie's been with the company over 14 years, plenty long enough to show the stuff he's made of.

"Eddie? Oh, he's okay. His bark is worse than his bite, you know. But he's all right underneath, if you *understand* him."

Now if that were the way people talked about me—whether I'd been with the company 14 years or 14 months—I'd consider myself a consummate flop. And I mean a *business* flop.

Two Sides to This Story

But of course there's another side to the story—Eddie's.

"Now, I don't like to gripe," says he, "but why does the office make all those silly *mistakes?*"

If you're foolish enough to ask him to explain, he can cite chapter and verse. That big order that was shipped a week late, six years ago come next June. The way the credit department writes sassy letters, just because an account is a little past due. And the correspondence department, why, if there's a single way to do things wrong that they haven't perfected into a science, Eddie's ready to eat his hat!

Doing It the Hard Way

Now, mind you, Eddie sells his share of merchandise. He earns enough to pay his bills. And he'll probably be right there at the same old stand, 10 or 15 years from now.

Well, maybe I'd better explain why I call him a complete flop. To begin with, Eddie is certainly earning his bread and butter the hard way. I think that's too obvious to require comment, for it's a pretty awful thing to go through life feeling that the boys (and girls) back home are letting you down, day after day, year after year.

How to Lose an Order

But more important, perhaps, than the strain on his morale and time, is the extra business he's losing every day.

He's losing business because you can't make a daily habit of telling "the gang" how little you think of them, and expect them to do those little, extra, friendly things that add up to so much.

Little Things That Don't Count

Little things like advising you that the new cub salesman has found a brand-new argument to use against competition. ("Eddie goes through the roof if we tell him what to say. Better wait till we test out that argument, and then send out a bulletin on it.")

Little things like asking Eddie's opinion on a new item for the line. ("Eddie's not the man to ask! He'll come back with a four-page letter telling us we aren't taking care of the business we've got!")

Little things like giving you a chance to collect that delinquent account, instead of starting suit. ("Eddie might get sore if we asked him," says the collection department head.)

Little things, you see, that really don't count—*not much!*

Eddie's Got a Real Complaint

Then there's the other side of the picture. O. K., this time Eddie has a real complaint! But does it get a fair hearing? Well, you remember the fable of the boy who spent his time crying, "Wolf! Wolf!" What happened when a wolf did appear on the scene?

Or maybe Eddie has a good suggestion, something that would perhaps mean a lot in his particular territory. It's hot. But who is to blame if there are two strikes against it from the start, simply because it comes from him? Not that anybody *means* to be prejudiced, but isn't Eddie always sending in suggestions, suggestions that everything be done a better way? So why get excited about one more?

A Smart Idea

Now, I know you've heard enough about Eddie, and that you're not living in the doghouse, as he is.

But have you ever stopped to think how smart it is to have an equally strong reputation, but in the *opposite direction?*

To have the folks back home say about you, "Bill's the guy to ask! He'll answer immediately. He *always* does!"

"Bill wouldn't claim commission on that account if it weren't fair; let's okay this right now!"

"Bill says this account is a good credit risk, so I'll ship without checking references. That will save two weeks."

—Not Much!

Little things, you see, by the dozen. No, they don't count— *not much!*

But there's really much more to this thing than meets the eye. Only the other day I heard of an incident that illustrates this very well.

Opportunity Knocks

A friend of mine who heads the sales department of a well-known company found himself with an unexpected promotion to make. The midwestern district sales manager had been severely injured in an auto mishap. Somebody had to take over.

"I went over the list of the 25 leading salesmen in our organization," he said. "Then I began to cull out. Several lacked the education desirable for leadership of an important group. A few fell because of age. On the plus side, due weight was given to appearance, ability to speak on their feet, and of course a sound record of steady, day-by-day production.

Three of a Kind

"Finally the list had boiled down to three names. From where I sat, there seemed little to choose between them. Any one of the three promised to make a top-drawer district sales manager!

"But I went one step further. I sent a memo to each department head in the company, simply listing these three names in alphabetical order, and saying, 'These three men are being considered for promotion to a sales executive post. Please advise which one of the three has had the best relations with your department.'

You'd Never Have Guessed It

"Well, I was in for a real surprise! These three men, who had stacked up like three peas in a pod up to this point, sure ranged all over the lot in company relations!

" 'Chronic complainer.' 'Uncooperative.' 'Sarcastic.' 'Our files show he always insists on his own way.' Well, that was the report on one of my fine candidates! Little was said either for or against the second.

"But the third drew a rare round of plaudits! 'Swell guy.' 'Seems to understand our department's problems.' 'We often call on him for local help, and he always comes through.' 'Has sent some very fine applicants for jobs with the company.' "

There's a Reason

The man who finally got the job that my friend had to fill really was chosen because of a lot of little things, the kind that don't count—*not much!*

A Salesman's Job Is to Sell

Now I don't want to give you the idea that it's become part of a salesman's job to win a popularity contest. On the contrary, I wouldn't be inclined to hire a man, much less promote him, if I thought he were either afraid, or too disinterested, to say his piece when he felt there was something wrong.

I'll go a step further. There *is* something wrong, every now and then, in the operations of every department of every concern. We're all human, and we all make mistakes.

Complain, But Don't Gripe

But there's a vast difference between a man who complains or criticizes occasionally, constructively, and fairly, and one who carries a chip on his shoulder, indulges in wisecracks in-

stead of statements of actual fact, and in general takes the attitude that it's the exception rather than the rule when things go right. Nine times out of ten, of course, it's only a habit. Maybe it started as an effort to be "smart." But like all habits, once it's started, it's liable to grow!

Maybe You Know This Man

I once asked a "gripe specialist" why, if he felt that way about his company, he didn't quit.

"No use," he answered readily, "the next spot would be just as bad. I know—I've been around!"

Well, at least he was honest about the matter! So then I said, "Who's your biggest customer, Tom?"

"Why, the Acme Company," he replied.

"Aren't they the people who are always asking special favors and running you ragged to keep them happy?"

"So what? You've got to overlook such things, you know, when an account gives you that much business!"

He Wouldn't Get the Point

Of course, I didn't ask Tom whether he had ever used the same philosophy in his attitude toward his biggest customer of all: the company that stands ready, day in and day out, to buy all he has to sell of professional skill, industry, and ability. No, there was no use asking that question. Tom wasn't a big enough man to get the point.

Do You Really Act on the Following Facts?

1. That "the house" is far and away your biggest customer? .... Yes_____ No_____

2. That it's becoming more and more important to "play ball with your biggest customer," since modern management has become aware of the cost of retaining a "prima-donna" type of salesman?. Yes_____ No_____

3. That, quite apart from management's attitude, a salesman's standing with the rank and file of the organization plays a very important part in his sales performance? .... Yes_____ No_____

4. That the "boys and girls" in the office, the shipping room, on the switchboard, and elsewhere, respond almost like magic to a friendly attitude on the part of any salesman? .... Yes_____ No_____

5. That, without meaning to, and often without realizing it, they do a lot of little "extras" for the friendly salesman, which in their totality mean a *lot* more business and a *lot* fewer headaches?.... Yes_____ No_____

6. That, although it's not part of selling to win a popularity contest, management must consider temperament, cooperativeness, and attitude before making promotions? .... Yes_____ No_____

7. That there's a *big* difference between registering constructive complaints and acting like a "gripe artist"? .... Yes_____ No_____

8. That the so-called "gripe artist" hardly ever gets an objective hearing on his suggestions or his legitimate criticisms, because he has built a reputation of always "going overboard" in his attitude?. Yes_____ No_____

9. That "playing ball with your biggest customer" doesn't mean that it's a good

thing to avoid all criticism of that customer? .... Yes____ No____

10. That the records show that men who
are considered "gripe artists" in one job
or with one company usually keep right
on complaining if placed in another job,
or with another company? .... Yes____ No____

Your score is _____

If you answered "yes" to only seven (or less) of the ten questions, you need a plan to improve your performance. Think it out
and write it out *now*, while you've got it in mind!

13

SMITH NEVER GETS
SMALL ORDERS!

Big Orders Are His Weakness

Not long ago I was visiting Joe Randall, who manages a sales force of about 150 men. As usual, we fell to talking about salesmen, and the selling habits and characteristics that mark the difference between men who ride on top and those who trail behind.

"I wonder if you can spot what's wrong with this man," said Randall, handing me a summary sheet of the previous month's business.

"Well, Joe," I said after a couple of minutes, "I may be wrong, but at a quick guess I'd say your man is off the beam because he's got a weakness for *big* orders!"

Joe nodded in agreement. "Haven't been able to break him of that habit—yet," he added.

Sure, Big Orders Are Fine

Now don't think for a minute that either Joe Randall or I don't *like* big orders! On the contrary, we both spend a lot of our time teaching men how to sell more of them.

But there's a right way and a wrong way of going about it, as there is in all other phases of selling. What we were discussing and criticizing was a man who was obviously off on the wrong tack.

You've Been Through It

Let me explain this by citing a mild case of this "ailment," such as you yourself have undoubtedly experienced if you've been in the field a few years.

You're selling, we'll say, a certain type of office equipment. Ten sales a month is what it takes to do a good job. And so you call on at least 100 prospects each month to find ten who will buy your unit. Occasionally you find one who can use two units, and you get a special kick out of writing the order.

Five Birds With One Stone

Then one day you run into a prospect who calmly tells you he might be interested in five!

Now it's at that moment, if you're a normal salesman, that something special is apt to happen to you. You begin to lose your perspective.

It Gets Under Your Skin

For example, your five-unit prospect asks you to come back next Tuesday at 11. You agree, of course, even though you had some excellent callbacks planned for that day in another part of your territory.

So you kill time next Tuesday from nine to 11, and then improvise some work for the afternoon. Your whole day's work, you see, really boils down to that one call. Now if you walk out with the order, you've won; you just wish you could do as well every Tuesday!

But chances are it isn't quite that easy. Big orders usually aren't. So you walk out empty-handed, having agreed to check back in a few days more, and you feel definitely low.

From Bad to Worse

Sure, it still looks like a good prospect, and you knew all along you probably wouldn't close the sale on that second call. Just the same, you had been *hoping*.

Well, the combination of that letdown together with your improvised plan for that afternoon doesn't work out well. And of course you've got to rearrange your plans for Wednesday, to take care of those calls you had originally planned for Tuesday.

Now You're on a Spot!

The next step is that you suddenly realize that you're low man so far for the month. Why, only a week ago you were confident you'd have a banner month, your 10 regular sales plus four "extras" on that *big* order!

So you say to yourself, "Well, I'd better land that big one, or the month will be a bust! I've put so much into it already, the only smart thing to do is to follow through and get it."

So you concentrate even more of your thinking and planning on this one prospect, which, of course, means that you're not paying your usual attention to your "bread-and-butter" type of work. Along toward the end of the month you *do* close your big sale! Of course, it's been cut down from five to three, and you begin to do some figuring.

You find that even counting the "big one," your total for the month is only seven! Yes, I'm sure it's happened to you, just as it has to me. You probably learned your lesson.

Peaks and Valleys Aren't Healthy

It simply isn't good salesmanship to work yourself into a spot where one, or a few, big prospects cause you to neglect your *regular* way of seeking business, which has, after all, done pretty well by you.

It isn't good salesmanship, either, to play the game so that a "yes" or "no" on one—or a few—big deal will make you or break you, not even for a month. You're too good a man, after all, to have even one conspicuously bad month.

It isn't good salesmanship, finally, to develop a "peak and valley" pattern in your work.

No, it never was good salesmanship to do those things—and *it never will be.*

There's a Simple Rule

Now I needn't tell you that the right way of handling big prospects is *not* to turn a fishy eye on them and say, "No thanks, I'm not interested." No, sir, you want to line up and follow up just as many of them as you can.

But in doing this, just make certain that you remember one simple rule: "It's the *total amount* of the business you write, not the size of individual orders, that pays the butcher and the baker!" So you want to do some plain talking to yourself as you line up and follow up the big ones. The trick, you see, is to avoid going about it in such a way that you'll end up with *less total business actually in the bag* than would have been the case if you'd never *met* your big prospects.

The Smartest Plan of All

I think you'll find it interesting and profitable to hear about the smartest plan I know of to achieve just that. This plan was developed by a man named Smith. But don't let that fool you. There's nothing run-of-the-mill about this chap except his name.

Smith Has His Ups and Downs

He's a very strong salesman, but when I first met him he had a "feast-or-famine" record that was enough to drive any sales manager to distraction. Sometimes he'd go a week or longer without a single sale, only to crash through with some spectacular business just as he was about to be "called on the carpet." And then, you could depend upon it, there would be another lapse.

Smith Never Gets a Small Order

"Don't let his record mislead you," said his sales manager. "He's a peak-and-valley artist, all right, but it isn't that he doesn't work every day. No, there's just one thing wrong with Smith. He never gets a small order!"

And so I talked with Smith. He agreed that his record of total business was very poor. He agreed that big orders alone somehow don't stack up so well unless they have small orders to keep them company.

You Can't Live on Cake Alone

"You're right," he said, when I pointed out that his was a problem of pacing, that no man can live on cake alone, that any man who sells only big orders must be deliberately passing up lots of small ones.

Still, I didn't think we'd gotten very far when the talk was all over.

There's a Turn in the Road

But I was in for a big surprise! Almost overnight, it seemed, Smith began to build one of those steady, day-by-day production records that marks the man who is habitually on top. Of course, I had to find out why. Such things don't go and happen by themselves!

A Word Does It

"There was really nothing you told me, that day a few weeks ago, that I hadn't known before," began Smith, in reply to my question. "But you did use one word that gave me an idea!"

"A word?" I was completely mystified.

"Yes, one word that seemed to show me a way to lick my problem. Remember? You said something about 'pacing.' "

I began to see a little daylight, but I didn't interrupt.

There's a Better Yardstick

"Well, that word made me realize, in a new sort of way, that all along I had been thinking of *prospects* I'd warmed up, and you were talking about *orders!*"

"Now you're getting hot!" I said. "Lining up prospects is an important part of the job, but it's the part that it's the easiest to kid yourself about! A man needs another yardstick to tell him how he's really doing."

"Yes, I was measuring each day's performance by one yardstick, but I saw that yours was a better one!"

He told me that the more he thought of it, the more sense there seemed to be in his new idea--the idea that he would plan all his work on the basis that he'd try never to let three consecutive days go by without actually writing an order!

There's Power in That Idea

Well, maybe you see the power behind that simple idea. It puts important things first; it's insurance against loss of perspective. It tells you when you're running short of warmed up prospects. Common sense then does the rest. It warns you when you're straying from the path of sound salesmanship, either in quest of "big prospects" at the expense of your regular way of seeking business, or for any other reason.

What a Man!

Yes, it's far and away the soundest approach I know to this problem of keeping your feet right on the ground, come what may.

But I mustn't forget to tell you. It's four years now since they stopped saying, "Smith never gets a small order."
Now they simply say, "What a salesman!"

SELF-OPERATING QUIZ

Do You Really Act on the Following Facts?

1. That a salesman's record that shows he gets *only* big orders really means that he's passing up small orders he should *also* get? .... Yes____ No____

2. That theoretically a record of only big orders is sound, but years of experience prove that any man who passes up the bread-and-butter type of order in his planning and solicitation patterns is taking a big chance, even if he "gets away with it"? .... Yes____ No____

3. That most salesmen are inclined to lose some of their normal perspective and judgment when an unusually big order is being considered? .... Yes____ No____

4. That if you don't successfully guard against this danger, a big order can cost you *lots* of sales volume and earnings, *even if you land it?* .... Yes____ No____

5. That the answer certainly isn't to "duck" big orders or big prospects, but to handle them in such a way that they don't throw you off balance? .... Yes____ No____

6. That "peak-and-valley" selling is never healthy? .... Yes____ No____

7. That there's one simple rule that will keep your thinking in balance on this point? .... Yes____ No____

8. That the best yardstick any salesman can use in checking on his day's performance is in terms of orders written, and not in terms of "prospects warmed up"? .... Yes____ No____

9. That every salesman should carefully think out his own proper pacing, decide how long it's safe for him to go between

orders, and then to rearrange whatever
is necessary to enable him to "work his
plan"? .... Yes___ No___

10. That such a plan warns you whenever
you're "going off the deep end," whether
in quest of "cake" alone, or for any other
reason? .... Yes___ No___

Your score is _____

If you answered "yes" to only seven (or less) of the ten questions, you need a plan to improve your performance. Think it out
and write it out *now*, while you've got it in mind!

14

SOME SALESMEN KNOW WHAT THE SCORE IS!

"It Can't Be Done"

Bud Hayes smiles whenever he talks about "the day I learned how to double my income."

And well he may! For on that day he joined the ranks of the fortunate, select few who have somehow come to see how easy a thing it is for each of us to rise to greater success and accomplishments, if we will but rid our minds of the belief that it can't be done.

Bud Had Life Figured Out

It all began in a very commonplace way. Bud, like most of us, had life figured out. You do the best you can, he reasoned, and if your success falls short of what you might like—well, what can you do about it? Some men get lucky breaks, and maybe it will be your turn some day!

Sometimes, of course, he would almost decide to put forth that extra effort by which every salesman knows he can increase his business 10 or maybe 15 per cent.

"But life's too short; it wouldn't be worth the effort," was the way he shrugged it off.

Then came the day when that answer would no longer do. Hospital bills have a way of mounting up, but Bud was grateful that his son pulled through.

An Idea Is Born

He went to see his local banker.

"How fast do you think you could pay off such a loan?" It was a natural question!

Well, Bud had figured beforehand. He knew the answer by heart. Income $15,000; family living expenses, payments on the house, on the car, on the insurance policy, incidentals—no, you couldn't make it more than $1,500 a year left over.

The banker looked at his figures. "Now if you could raise your income by $1,500 this year, you could pay off the whole $3,000 in the next 12 months, couldn't you?"

"Why, yes!"

Bud Had Never Thought of It

Now Bud had never thought of it that way before. That $1,500, before the illness, was really the "spending money" in his life! A 10 per cent increase in his sales would really double it!

Well, here was only the first step, and the least important one, in Bud's story. What happened next brought him a lot more than that extra $1,500, and brought it in cash, too.

An Unexpected Reward

For Bud learned a very important lesson, as he tightened up on his selling habits to get that extra 10 per cent. He learned that whenever a salesman does that, there's an unexpected dividend that results.

It works this way. As Bud polished up his sales talk, his closing strategy, and so on, he began to notice that this extra power applied not only to the 10 per cent additional prospects that he had to sell, but permeated his whole selling program.

Tools Have Many Uses

That new sales point he worked up to turn a "no" into a "yes" automatically served to turn the *easy* orders into *bigger* ones!

You never saw a more surprised man in your life than Bud when he realized that his effort to increase his sales by 10 per cent really resulted in an increase that was fourfold as large!

Nothing Succeeds Like Success

Yet Bud had only stumbled on a principle as old as humanity itself. I don't know how old is the slogan, "Nothing succeeds like success." I do know that if this principle and the slogan that expresses it didn't operate with the certainty that marks the rising and the setting of the sun, then every successful man you know would still be at the bottom of the ladder.

NOTHING
SUCCEEDS
LIKE
SUCCESS

It's a Small Step to a New World

You can't make a genuine and intelligent effort at self-improvement without achieving at least some progress. And note this well: Even the smallest step forward in terms of self-betterment is often the sole difference between a big man and a small one, between a success and a failure. Don't ask me why, but I've seen it happen far too often to permit of any doubt.

Facts and Figures

If 20 per cent of the salesmen sell 80 per cent of the goods and services sold in America, that leaves only 20 per cent of the rewards of selling to be shared by 80 per cent of those who sell.

That's something to think about! Yes, something to ponder before you decide a 10 per cent increase in selling power wouldn't be worth the effort.

You Don't Know Your Own Power

I often think how many lives would be transformed if every salesman somehow came to understand his own power. So few of us do! Of those who do, how many have to find it out the hard way!

Red Had the Answers

Take Red Hamilton, for example. He was perfectly content to go on day after day, doing about an average job. When something turned up now and then that should have served to prod him, he indulged in the usual excuses and alibis.

I don't think you'd ever guess what it was that finally blasted him out of his rut.

Fate Takes a Hand

Well, let's call it fate that caused Red to run into Dan Humphries, whom he hadn't seen since Dan shipped off to fight the war. They went to lunch, of course. Dan, it developed as they talked, was doing pretty well. With his savings and a GI loan, he had gone into business for himself.

Some Day We'll Go to Town

"Lucky dog!" said Red, as he heard this piece of news. "Remember the days before the war, when you were just a salesman, like me, working your head off for someone else? Remember how often we used to say that some day we'd find a way to set up for ourselves and really go to town? Now you *are* in business for yourself!"

"Well, Red," said Dan, "I've learned a few things since those days, and here's one that ought to be of interest to you. You may not realize it—I know I didn't—but right this minute, you are in business for yourself, just as much as I am!

It's Fun to Put One Over

"Oh, no, I'm not batty! It's really very simple. For example, in the old days, if you and I took off an afternoon to see a ball game, well, we were pretty sure of one thing! We were pretty sure we were putting one over on the company!"

"Yes, but . . ." began Red.

"Now wait a minute, mister," interrupted Dan. "Take me, for instance. I haven't got a boss. I could take off every afternoon in the week. *But do I?*"

It Takes a Little Thinking

"You've got a point there, but you're overdoing it!" Had it been anyone but an old buddy shooting off his mouth, Red might have gotten sore at this nonsense.

But you can't argue with facts, especially if the other fellow knows what he's talking about. So it wasn't long before Red stopped arguing and began to enthuse about Dan's idea.

"So you've got to hand in records and reports," Dan explained. "Well, so do I! To the bank and to the government—and they make yours look like child's play!

"And you've got to sell at prices fixed by your company. Well, do you think I can set any price I want? No, sir, it's cost and competition that set my prices, just like yours!

You Can Write Your Own Ticket

"Sure, I'm making a lot more money today than I did as a salesman! But do you want to know something? If I'd realized in the old days that I was really in business for myself, that every time I cut a corner, it was coming out of my pocket—if I'd gone into a brain-sweat when business wasn't right, the way I do today—well, if I'd known what the score was in those days, my checks would have been as big then as the money I'm earning today!"

A Milestone in Red's Life

There was a new spring in Red's step, a new look on his face, a new erectness to his shoulders as he walked home that night. That afternoon had been a milestone in his life. For the first time in 12 long years of selling he had really done his *best!*

How could it be otherwise? Red, you see, for the first time in 12 years, had really learned the score!

It's Yours for the Asking

There's one thing more I'd like to mention about this matter of success. It's more than a matter of dollars and cents, more than volume of sales and money to spend or save. Much more.

There's something about doing the best job you're capable of that no amount of money could ever buy. I can't name it, and I'm not going to try. It's a way of life that includes self-respect, finding fun instead of a chore in each hour's work, and the satisfaction that comes from making progress.

It's a way of life, I might add, that can be yours any day you wish to begin.

SELF-OPERATING QUIZ

Do You Really Act on the Following Facts?

1. That if a salesman increases his income by 10 per cent, he probably is increasing his "spending money" or "saving money" by 100 per cent? .... Yes_____ No_____
2. That a 10 per cent increase in selling effectiveness has a twofold effect, which means an increase of perhaps 50 per cent in total sales? .... Yes_____ No_____
3. That there's plenty of truth in the age-old maxim, "Nothing succeeds like success"? .... Yes_____ No_____
4. That you can't make a genuine and intelligent effort at self-improvement without achieving at least *some* progress?... Yes_____ No_____
5. That often only a small step forward is the sole difference between a "small" man and a "big" man? .... Yes_____ No_____
6. That 20 per cent of the salesmen in America sell 80 per cent of the orders, leaving only 20 per cent of the reward to be spread among 80 per cent of the men? .... Yes_____ No_____
7. That most of us don't "know our own power"? .... Yes_____ No_____
8. That every salesman is in effect "in business for himself"? .... Yes_____ No_____
9. That a salesman who goes into business for himself and increases his income usually does so because once he's "on his own" he works harder and cuts fewer corners than formerly? .... Yes_____ No_____
10. That doing the best job you are capable of has important rewards in addition to those measurable in dollars? .... Yes_____ No_____

Your score is _____

If you answered "yes" to only seven (or less) of the ten questions, you need a plan to improve your performance. Think it out and write it out *now*, while you've got it in mind!

15

CHAMPIONS DON'T
JUST HAPPEN

Three Is Lucky

"Three is my lucky number," said Bill Carr with a smile, as he and I settled down to seats number three and four in the Pullman car.

I had heard him say that before, and had wondered just what he meant. In answer to my question, what a story I got! It thrilled me then, and it has thrilled almost every salesman I've told it to since—old-timers as well as novices.

"You see," Bill began, "I've been selling all my life. Greatest game in the world—if you're good, that is!"

"Wouldn't be happy at anything else, would you, Bill?" I agreed.

There's Always a Bottleneck!

"No, but years ago, before this 'lucky three' you asked about, I had more headaches than fun out of my work. It took three selling jobs, you see, before I discovered how to be a winner. Three jobs before I learned that every selling job has a bottleneck, and that until you lick it, you just scrape along."

I urged him to explain.

"My first try," he replied, "was in life insurance. After a year or so I was sure I'd do better selling a tangible, so I switched to automobiles. Then when I discovered I wasn't exactly a world-beater selling cars, I decided that my meat was a resale article. So I nodded fast when I was offered a chance to sell automobile accessories. 'Here,' I told myself, 'is where I'll really go places.'"

"And then you broke all records," I interrupted, knowing his success in that line.

How It All Started

"Not at first, I didn't!" Bill shot back. "Not until I sat down one evening, tired and discouraged, about ready to admit that as a salesman I could make a bare living, but not much more.

"Then all at once I had a bright idea. I got to thinking that out of my 50 or 60 customers, there were about six who seemed to buy all they could from me each time I called. Pet accounts —you know, every salesman has a few like that.

" 'Bill, old boy,' I said to myself, 'if those accounts could use *twice* as much of your line as they now do, they'd be tickled to death to give you the extra business. Now how are you going to go about it to put them in that spot?'

Bill Figures It Out

"Well, it didn't take long to figure out at least a few things I could do right off. Take that Jones account. Mr. Jones always gave me an order, with the result that I let him worry about how he was going to resell what he bought. Why, it was months since I had had a session with Jones' salesmen, to tell them how to resell our line. In those months, what had happened? Simply this: Jones had put on a couple of new men who probably knew nothing about our line; competition had come out with some hot improvements; my own company had brought out new products too!

"So it hit me like the proverbial ton of bricks. The bottleneck I had to smash was whatever stood in the way of increased resale volume of my line!"

Don't Stop There!

"Nice work!" I interrupted. "Go on, Bill, don't stop there!"

"Well," Bill carried on, "before long I was on top all right, because I applied my new idea to as many accounts as I could. But there was one thing that bothered me now and then. Every time the home office played me up as a 'hotshot' salesman, I'd remember the tough going I'd had in insurance and automobiles. Would I have to go back to slim pickings if for some reason I had to give up my present work?

You Know the Answer

"But of course you know the answer," Bill concluded. "In time I figured out what I should have realized at the start. *Every* selling job has its bottleneck! As for insurance, in my particular area the difficulty had been that people 'thought small.' Now if I had realized that quite clearly while I was on that job, I know I could have licked that 'bottleneck.'

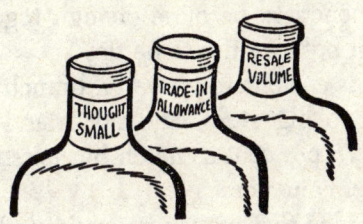

"As for selling cars, it was clear as crystal to me, in retrospect, that the bottleneck had been the prospects' oblivion to everything except the amount of the trade-in allowance. 'Why,' I found myself thinking, 'if I were back selling cars today, I'd have no difficulty at all in figuring out—and licking—that particular bottleneck, either!'

It Took Three Tries

"That's the whole story, I guess." Bill was silent for a long moment, and then added, "Don't ask me why, but that experience, years ago, seemed to make three my 'lucky number.' It took three tries—although it needn't have!—for me to get the one idea that marked the road to success. Because, by golly, you know as well as I do that the woods are full of salesmen who have the ability to be winners but who limp along in second speed simply because they've never figured out exactly what single thing constitutes the old bottleneck on their particular job!"

Yes, I knew that as well as Bill did, and if you'll think it over you too will agree that his story applies to *all* selling.

It May Be Time

I know a chap whose bottleneck was time. He sells housewares to department stores in larger cities, and for years his routine was to "kill" several hours each day after he'd called on his one customer in that town, waiting for transportation to the next. Five calls a week, regular as clockwork, except when two large cities happened to be close enough together so that he could work them both on the same day.

Then one of his customers opened a branch store in a lively town between two big cities, and my friend was amazed to find that he got 75 per cent as much business from the branch store as from the main store.

So he got the idea that maybe he could find and work some lively small town each day in addition to his big city account.

Silly that he hadn't thought of that before, since it increased his income from about average to 50 per cent above average? Not any sillier than the bottlenecks most of us fail to spot and cope with!

It May Be Competition

I know a fellow whose Nemesis was nothing more nor less than the fact that his territory was dominated by an old, respected competitor, while he was trying to put over a new line. His line was hot, but what good did that do if he couldn't get a chance to prove it?

Call after call he ran into the same old brushoff: "Sorry, we sell the Smith line, and are quite satisfied with it. Good day."

Yes, it seemed quite clear that he'd go right on picking up the crumbs, and all because of *one* obstacle—that big competitor.

Then one day, in sheer exasperation, he tried a new approach. Knowing full well that his next prospect would be a Smith user, he opened up with, "Mr. Prospect, I suppose you use the Smith line, and are quite satisfied with it."

"That's right!"

The Worm Turns

"Well, maybe you've never even heard of the house I represent—we're new down here—and we'd be wasting our time if we tried to break into this territory without having something mighty attractive to offer. I'd like two or three minutes to tell you the story, and I think I can guarantee you a pleasant surprise!"

Well, the buyer was human, wasn't he? What could he do, when here was a brash salesman who boldly took the wind out of his standard brush-off that he used on all competitors of the Smith Company?

Funny that my friend didn't think of that a lot earlier, seeing how obvious it is and how much heartache he could have spared himself if he had!

But it's not a bit funnier than the unsmashed bottleneck that may be plaguing you.

Hindsight Makes It Easy

Yes, there's one peculiar thing about this business of finding and smashing the bottleneck that's holding back a man on any particular selling job. It is that in retrospect the whole thing always seems so simple and obvious. Probably that's just what causes some men to say, when I tell them Bill Carr's story, "That's swell. I like it. But it just doesn't apply to my work. You see, my obstacle is price, and I can't change *that*."

Or, "Well, I'd like to see Bill Carr or anyone else use that idea to up business in my line. My big problem is that all the people who really need our equipment have already got it, and I've got to work on the fringe prospects."

Or, "Mine is a callback deal, and there's not much I can do till I've got a prospect warmed up so he's ready to close."

Or any one of a dozen similar reasons.

Let's Take a Good Look

But I think each and every one of these men, in spite of his sincerity, is actually proving, day in and day out, that Bill's story does apply in their respective cases, rather than the reverse. I think I can prove it to anyone with an open mind.

"Brother," I say, "let's look into this thing together, frankly. I'll grant that your obstacle is what you say it is: price, or fringe prospects, or a callback deal, or whatever you yourself have diagnosed it to be. You *ought* to know, and even if you happen to be wrong, the fact that that particular obstacle stacks up in your mind as your big hurdle makes it just that.

"So we're agreed on the first point. Let's proceed to the second. How many dollars or units would you have to sell each month in order to do a topflight job—one that both you and your boss would call really good?"

"Twenty units a month," comes the answer.

"Okay! Now, how many are you averaging?"

A little reflection, and then, "Eleven—probably 12 a month, this last year or so."

How Come?

"Well, just one thing more. How come, if your problem is price, or fringe prospects, that you are able to find and close 12 a month? I mean, the fact that you do sell 144 a year proves pretty conclusively that your product is salable in your territory. Those 144 buyers weren't wrong, were they? Nor in some sort of class or group by themselves, that happens to be just that size? You don't really think, do you, that it would be actually impossible for you to enlarge that group, if you really sharpen up your tools, so that you could count 240 where you now have 144?"

No, I fail to see any magic limitation to 12 a month on *that* man's job. For, as I say, if his obstacle is so real that it's valid against the extra eight, then I don't see how he manages to sell the 12 he *is* selling.

The Salesman Sold Himself

What I do see in that picture is something quite different. I see a salesman who "sold himself" on the idea that although 20 is the goal he'd like to shoot at, he'll settle for 12, because to add the other eight he'd have to part with the brainsweat that is the price of applying Bill Carr's idea to his own job.

And maybe it's just as well, after all. I suppose if every salesman scored "20" instead of "12," the world wouldn't pay that extra measure of respect and compensation it gladly tenders champions.

Hundreds Have Heard It

But, as I said, I've told Bill Carr's story to hundreds of sales-men, novices and old-timers and those in between. I've seen the great majority applaud it, and of these a good percentage apply it to their own day-by-day work. And finally, of those who did that, I've yet to see a single man who regretted it.

As long as that holds true, I'll go on telling it at every oppor-tunity.

Wouldn't you?

Self-operating Quiz

Do You Really Act on the Following Facts?

1. That *every* selling job has a "bottle-neck"? .... Yes____ No____

2. That until a salesman licks his particular "bottleneck" he just manages to scrape along? .... Yes____ No____

3. That only a few salesmen ever actually determine just what it is that is holding them back in their selling? .... Yes____ No____

4. That a peculiarity about "bottlenecks" is that once you lick yours, you begin to wonder why you didn't do it long ago, since it's all so simple? .... Yes____ No____

5. That any salesman who says that the "bottleneck" principle doesn't apply to him is ducking behind an alibi?........ Yes____ No____

6. That if you are now selling *x* units or orders a month in your territory, that fact in itself is pretty conclusive proof that you could improve your score if you could just overcome your chief selling obstacle? .... Yes____ No____

7. That the price for doing this is that you must part with some "brainsweat" to accomplish it? .... Yes____ No____

8. That the fact that most salesmen won't make this additional effort means that those who do reap a generous measure of extra reward? .... Yes____ No____

9. That the records show that if any salesman really gets to work on this principle, he's bound to be ahead of the game?... Yes____ No____

10. That the first step is to *identify* accurately just what your own "bottleneck" is? .... Yes____ No____

Your score is _____

If you answered "yes" to only seven (or less) of the ten questions, you need a plan to improve your performance. Think it out and write it out *now*, while you've got it in mind!

16

SURE, I'M LUCKY!

Three Can't Live as Cheaply as One

Jack Beaver is one lucky guy. "Sure, I'm lucky!" he's always ready to admit.

And why? Take, for example, the girl he married. Now lots of young men marry fine girls, but how many find that, in addition to everything else, the girl of their choice has good sales sense?

Well, Mary Beaver had, but it wasn't until they'd been married a couple of years that she put her talent to full use. It all came about when Jack and Mary discovered that three can't live as cheaply as one.

Jack Turns On the Heat

Of course, Jack turned on the heat, making a couple of extra calls each day, and planning his work as he had never done before. But in spite of the additional business this brought him, he still found it difficult to keep up with family expenses, payments on the house, his life insurance premiums, and all the incidentals.

Now the truth is that if it hadn't been for something special in his case, Jack Beaver would doubtless have scraped along—saving a dollar here, earning an extra dollar there, and somehow getting by, as many others do.

But there was this special factor in Jack's case, and, try as he would, he couldn't duck it. He had told himself all along that if he ever went all out for volume he could sell as much as any man in the group. Well, here he was, pounding away for all he was worth, yet he found that his best pace didn't push him up beyond the middle of the list.

They Know the Answers

"How do some of the top men do it?" inquired Mary one day, when Jack confessed that he wasn't in the money on a sales contest he had tried so hard to win.

"They must know some of the answers that I don't know," he replied.

"Like what?"

"Oh, I don't know. Now take Tom Farrell, for instance. Been with the company 22 years. Knows every screw and bolt in our machine by its first name. And he knows our competitors' products just as well. You can't learn that stuff overnight, you know. It takes years!"

"I see." Mary was up to something. Jack could tell by the expression on her face.

"But I know our product as well as most of the men do," Jack hastened to add. "Enough to sell it, any day in the week."

"Jack, you never studied biology, did you? Well then, let me tell you . . ."

Mary Tells a Story

Mary told the story of the bright student of biology who was greatly honored by being appointed laboratory assistant to a world-famous biologist.

His first assignment was the dissection of a fish. He labored far into the night to do an outstanding job.

Next day, proud of his performance, he entered the good doctor's study. He grew impatient as the latter chatted about one thing and another, and seized the first opportunity to mention the job he had completed so laboriously.

"Oh, the fish?" answered the biologist. "Study it for another day or two; it's an interesting specimen."

Now that particular fish was the last thing in the world the younger man ever wanted to see again. But what could he do?

There's That Fish Again!

And, so goes the story, a couple of days later, the doctor once again put off his eager assistant, "That's really a very interesting specimen. Let's see what you discover in the next day or so."

It was on this third tussle with the fish that the bright young student made a discovery that won him wide acclaim!

"It's a true story, Jack," Mary concluded, "and I think the same method ought to find sales points as well as biological data."

Of course, it would have been just a bunch of conversation if Jack hadn't been disturbed about that middle-of-the-group pace of his. As it was, within a week he learned more about his product than in the preceding two years.

The Fish Story Pays Off

The amazing thing was, not only how much he hadn't known, but how significant much of his new sales ammunition was. "Why, they told me that when I was being trained two years ago, but it didn't seem important then!" and, "Golly, now I can prove to anyone that our unit will last longer than our competitors'!"

Yes, overnight it seemed, Jack propelled himself out of the group who try to sell by talking generalities like "Less expensive to maintain," "Easier to operate," and so on. He had joined the group who have the knowledge that enables them not only to make specific claims, but also to back up each one with fact and demonstration showing *how* and *why* that claim is *accurate, important,* and *unique.*

Every Sales Point Is Important

But don't let me give you the impression that it's only *product* information that merits proper study.

I once sat in on a dramatic tussle between prospect and

salesman that illustrates, better than anything else I can think of, how important a sales point of any type can be. Yes, I remember the incident vividly, though it occurred almost 20 years ago. I was visiting a friend, a shoe manufacturer with a bustling factory near Boston.

We had been chatting along, as old friends will, when Cole's secretary reminded him that he had an appointment with a Mr. White, who had just arrived.

"Stay where you are," said Ned Cole to me, "and in a few minutes we'll go to lunch. I won't give this salesman—what's-his-name, White?—more than a few minutes."

"Take all the time you need," I replied. "I'm in no hurry, you know."

Price Isn't Everything

"Well," answered my friend, "you're interested in everything having to do with selling, so I'll tell you about this appointment. This fellow White sells a fabric that we use in large quantities, but we buy it from another house. Yesterday he called and asked for a few minutes. His price is attractive, but we're going to stick with our old suppliers. I'll give him his few minutes, but that's all there's to it."

As White and I were introduced I felt a bit sorry for him. How long would it take him, I wondered, to recognize that he couldn't open this particular account?

"Mr. Cole," he began, "you may recall that on my previous visit I explained why we could quote a rather attractive price on our product."

"Yes, I remember," answered Cole, polite but obviously not encouraging.

"And I mentioned that we have been selling our product to some good companies in your field for quite a few years."

"Oh, I know. I really don't doubt you have a reliable line. But really, Mr. White, we have decided. . . ."

Then it happened.

There's One More Fact

White interrupted, "But there's one more fact I wanted to give you, Mr. Cole. There's one piece of information I guess you haven't got, because it has developed since our last talk."

"And what's that?"

"Did you happen to hear that about two weeks ago the Hi-Stile Shoe Company switched to us?"

"No, as a matter of fact I didn't," said Cole, his tone and manner indicating just a shade of interest.

"Yes, they've switched all right, after holding out all this time."

The Prospect Is All Ears

"What do you mean by 'holding out'?" asked my friend. He seemed to be listening with *both* ears now!

"Well," answered White, "they have been using the same

supplier you have, for 10 to 15 years, just like you. And they wanted to stay put, I guess. Felt loyal to the house after all those years."

I felt the drama of the situation as Cole then asked, "White, do you happen to know *why* they changed houses? If it isn't confidential, I mean. . . ."

White measured up to the situation like a master. "Mr. Cole," he said, "there's absolutely nothing confidential about it. Like you, they build a lot of shoes in the course of a year. A small saving per pair makes a big difference on a volume operation.

"Let's assume that you, Mr. Cole, make 10,000 pairs a month. Let's see, that's 120,000 pairs a year! Now it won't take you over one minute to save a cool $4,800 in your costs. Just tell me when to start shipping!"

As Cole left the office to talk with one of his associates, I asked White an obvious question, "Tell me, did you really hope to get this account by telling your story about Hi-Stile?"

It's All in Knowing How

"I felt I had a pretty good chance, although I couldn't be sure, of course. Maybe I was optimistic because I've just opened two other accounts with that same sales point, and there are a few more I'm going after too."

Perhaps I showed my astonishment at this reply. I urged him to give me the full story.

"This is my third call on Mr. Cole," he began. "He passed me up the first time, although I showed him he could make a saving by using our product. My predecessor in this territory had told him the same story before, I guess. Anyway, there didn't seem to be any news in my story, and it didn't get him to change suppliers.

"Next time I gave him a rather impressive list of competitors who have used our product for ten years or more. Same result. These manufacturers don't change suppliers on impulse, and I guess Mr. Cole figured that if some had used *us* for years, why, he and others had used *his* house for years too—so what?

News Can Be Dramatized

"So I figured that probably the news of a *new* account might be a stronger testimonial than the story of old accounts, not only for this company, but for these others I've been trying to swing over since I came into the territory. I figured that that would probably make them wonder *why* one of their competitors had switched at this particular time.

"So I just kept calling on these half-dozen accounts, knowing that regardless of which one I got first, I could use the event as a strong sales point because it was a new one!"

You see it isn't only product information that yields sales points. Oftener than we are apt to realize there's a whopper of a sales point in the morning headlines, in the magazine article we read for relaxation, in the casual objection of a prospect, in the new law Congress is debating; or in the new policy announced by a competitor, which, although adopted to create an advantage for *him*, may easily create an "angle" for *you*.

Sales Points Are Precious

Yes, for all of us who earn our living by selling, the most precious of all possessions are those facts that, skillfully used, impel the prospect or the customer to conclude that the proper answer is, "O. K., I'll buy."

Obviously we can't have too many of them—good ones, that is.

And yet, do we really make the most of our opportunities in this respect? Let's face the facts. Take a group of, say, 20 men selling the same product for the same house. I'll wager that you'll find that each man has his own little group of sales points, and that not *one* in the group uses, or even really understands, all the points used by all the men. Nor half of them, for that matter!

What's the Reason?

Why? Aren't they all good? Well, each man makes a living with his own selection from the ensemble, so there must be some power in *those*. And so on with the points each of the others use in their particular work.

But I think I know the answer to all this. Jack Beaver was lucky, if you ask me, because his wife had studied biology. For it was her story about "the fish" that showed him the proper, the fruitful way of seeking selling points.

Don't ask me why, but I've noticed throughout the years that the sales ammunition that really "wows" the prospects is always knowledge or an idea that we come by the hard way.

Call it concentration, or vision, or alertness, or what you will, in either case there's a price that must be paid.

Salesman White didn't get those new accounts without beating out a new mental path marked "This way to a sales point worth five new customers." Jack Beaver thought he had most of the answers until he bothered to check up.

You and I Must Pay Too

You and I must pay the price too, either the price of mediocrity or the price of hewing out our own success. Yes, it takes industry really to know your product, just as it takes imagination to see that the acquisition of one new account can be made a selling point with power behind it. And all the way between these two extremes—all the way between sales points that are literally built into your product and sales points that are based on the day's news—all the way in between, I repeat, there are sales points almost beyond number, waiting to be discovered and put to work.

But make no mistake about one thing. There is an art of

learning as well as an art of teaching. No type of training course or manual or sales meeting has yet been devised that will do the salesman's *thinking* and *understanding* for him. Nor is there ever likely to be!

"WANTED: A dozen new sales points." What a challenge to those of us who think the going's tough!

Do You Really Act on the Following Facts?

1. That many men who tell themselves, "I could be top man if I wanted to put in all the extra effort," really aren't equipped with the necessary product information to get to the top by simply working harder at *selling*? .... Yes____ No____

2. That studying product information is much more profitable after you've been out selling than it possibly can be when you're new on the job, since you then have enough background to appreciate the importance of each point? .... Yes____ No____

3. That it is only by making such a systematic and periodic review that a salesman can find out which points he has forgotten, or which he never really understood, or which he never really appreciated? .... Yes____ No____

4. That such a program is the only means by which you can develop the specific claims and the proof to back them up that is the mark of topflight selling?.... Yes____ No____

5. That this principle applies to *all* information that has sales value, and not only to *product* information? .... Yes____ No____

6. That sometimes the testimonial value of a *new* account is greater than that of a list of *old* ones? .... Yes____ No____

7. That every sales point is a precious possession, whether it's about something that's literally built into your product or something developed from this morning's headlines? .... Yes____ No____

8. That if ten men are selling the same product, no two of them will use exactly the same list of sales points, and that the man on top is very likely the one who has taken the time and effort to develop the *longest* list of all? .... Yes____ No____

9. That the principle illustrated by the "fish
   story" coincides with the realities of selling, since the best sales ammunition is
   almost always obtained by the constant
   plugging and perseverance that scien-
   tists use to obtain their new information? Yes_____ No_____

10. That there is an art of learning as well
    as an art of teaching, and that no one
    can be taught unless he is ready to
    learn? .... Yes_____ No_____

    Your score is _____

If you answered "yes" to only seven (or less) of the ten questions, you need a plan to improve your performance. Think it out
and write it out *now,* while you've got it in mind!

17

"YES" IS A 15-LETTER
WORD

Tom Wishes He Were Twins!

Tom Wilson lives near me and we often see each other on the morning train going into the city.

"How's business, Tom?" I asked the other day, as we settled down in our seats.

I asked the question rather casually, because Tom is a top-flight salesman, and his usual answer to that particular query is "Great! Only wish I were twins, so I could make more calls!"

But on this occasion his reply was less enthusiastic. "Oh, I've seen it better. Prospects seem to be stalling a lot lately. Maybe it's the weather, or politics, or Lord-knows-what. Don't know why, but it's tough to get a 'yes'!"

"Well, 'yes' is a 15-letter word," I commented, more by way of consolation than anything else.

"Now there's one you'll have to explain," said Tom. "Sounds like a new slant. What's it all about?"

Every Prospect Has Five Questions

So I pointed out to my companion that, as I see it, there are five questions that any prospect or buyer must answer in the affirmative before he's ready to be closed.

"And those five silent 'yesses' count up to 15 letters, Tom. Get the idea?"

"Oh, sure, I can do simple arithmetic! Only thing that bothers me is just what are those five questions?"

Well, I'd asked for it, so I decided to begin at the beginning.

"I'll name them in a minute, Tom, but first let me explain that I don't mean that a prospect is necessarily *aware* of these particular questions, or that they hit him in any particular order. What I do mean is that they're always there in the background, ready to spoil a sale. What's more, every time a sale is lost, you can bet your last dollar it's because the prospect decided 'no' on at least one of them."

Tom Gets the Big Idea

"So you mean," interrupted Tom, "that in the case of each one of these prospects I mentioned, the reason has to be somewhere among those five points?"

"Exactly!" I agreed. "You've got the swing of it now. As I run through the list, you check me and see if I'm not right."

"Shoot."

"O. K., here's for Number One. Have any of these prospects put you off either by sending out word they were too busy to see you, or by telling you they weren't interested as you began your presentation? Yes? Well, I'm leading up to something important, but first, do you see that in those cases you lost out because the prospect decided 'no' on the first question: 'Shall I give this salesman an opportunity to tell his story?' "

"Sure, but . . ."

No Story—No Sale

"Now keep your shirt on, Tom, and you'll see what I'm driving at. Maybe you happened in at a bad time; maybe you didn't open up with a real punch. But whatever the reason, the point is that neither you nor I can ever make the sale if the prospect decides the wrong way on that question. Since this is so, the least any salesman can do, when he finds that happening to him oftener than it should, is to check up on his technique for getting a hearing."

Tom lit a cigarette as he pondered the matter. "You've got a point, all right," he finally replied, "and I guess every salesman knows things he can do to avoid that type of brush-off. Haven't thought along those lines for quite a while. Well, what's Question Number Two?"

Here's Number Two

"Now that one is easier to explain," I continued. "Some sales are lost because the prospect decides, after listening to the story, that he doesn't need the type of goods or services being offered. But let me clarify one thing right here. I'm talking about a case where the prospect decides, rightly or wrongly, that he doesn't need *anybody's* typewriter, or *any* make of truck, not merely the typewriter or the truck *you* happen to be selling."

"Well, that's the same thing, isn't it? Maybe I'm still sleepy, but if he decides he doesn't want any, that includes me out too, doesn't it?"

There's a Big Difference

"Not by a long shot, Tom," I retorted. "Look at it this way. I remember a case where a glove salesman and a buyer got really peeved with one another, simply because the salesman kept on trying to show that his product was the best seller on the market, while the prospect kept repeating that he didn't need any of the stuff.

"Now," I continued, "if that salesman had been smart, he would have realized that he and the buyer were really talking about two entirely different things. He would have realized that his job was to show the buyer that he could use some *gloves,* not *his* brand, but just *gloves.* He should have pointed out that although the store glove inventory was a bit heavy, the buyer could easily place an order for delivery 30 days later.

That's Exactly What Happened

"As a matter of fact, that's exactly the solution they arrived at, when the assistant glove buyer happened along and made the suggestion. But that sale was made in spite of the salesman, not because of him, as I see it. Oh, there's many a sale muffed because the salesman is so intent on selling his own line or product that he doesn't see that the real obstacle is Question Number Two: 'Shall I buy anybody's line or product today?' "

"Say, there's a point I like," commented Tom. "Now what's for Number Three?"

Here's Your Old Friend—Competition

"Number Three," I answered, "needs no explanation at all. It belongs on the list, of course, because without a 'yes' on this one there's certainly no sale. It's simply this: The prospect has got to decide whether he wants *your* product, or service, or line, or whether he prefers a competitor's."

"That's *one* of the five questions that no salesman is ever likely to forget, I guess! O. K., you needn't explain that one, but I'll jot it down with the others, so that my list will be complete."

Look Out for This One!

"Number Four coming up, then," I carried on, "and it's one that trips up many a sale. Every prospect, you'll agree, must say 'yes' to this one before he can buy: 'Have I decided which model, or what quantities, or which accessory items I'd buy if I did place the order?' "

"Yes, I follow that," interrupted Tom. "But why do you say it trips up many a sale?"

"Because all too often that's one of the fuzzy points in a prospect's mind, so he's inclined to decide 'no.'

"Let's take a reasonably typical case. Salesman Jones hurdles the first three questions. He gets the interview, he establishes the need, he convinces the prospect that his product is the one to buy.

The Salesman Won't Talk

"Then what? He's purposely a little vague as to the model or size or quantities he'd recommend. If he shoots too high, he'll lose out; if he aims too low, he's missing the real opportunity. So Buyer Smith is supposed to decide 'yes' on Question Number Four without benefit of help or advice. Small wonder that he often decides 'no' instead!

"Or take the other extreme. Salesman White may be so insistent in his recommendations that Prospect Smith may hesitate between his own judgment and the advice he's being pressed to accept.

"Now I'm not going to tell you, Tom, how to handle the situation, but I think you'll agree that the prospect must decide 'yes' on this question before he can say, 'Sign me up.'"

A Point Worth Noting

"No argument there. As a matter of fact, that's a point I can use on my very first call this morning! But look, we're almost, at our station. Let's get to the fifth question; I want to have a complete list so I can refer to it again."

"O. K., Question Five is another old friend: 'Shall I buy to-day?' Like Number Three, it's one that salesmen are constantly aware of, but it belongs on the list to make it complete.

"Well, we're in. Let me know, Tom, if our little discussion helps you get some of those '15-letter words'!"

Now I don't know yet what Tom Wilson's experience will be, but there are quite a few salesmen who have found this approach a big help.

How About You?

Probably you too, with a little thought, will find that there are one or two of these five points that highlight your own selling problem. Once you've got them out in the open, it's almost always a simple matter to find and use the proper corrective.

Now just to show you what a completely practical approach this is, I'd like to tell you of an unusual case—unusual because the salesman found he had to tighten up not on one or a few, but on *all five* points.

Green Grabs a Tough One

I'll admit that this man—I'll call him Jim Green—took on a very tough assignment.

His company decided that they wanted to set up a leased department arrangement with certain leading department stores. You know, a deal where the manufacturer puts in the merchandise and personnel, and pays the store a percentage on sales made in that department.

Well, when I met Green he was 'way down in the dumps. Four months of hard work, without a single deal closed! And to make it worse, without any that looked as though they *might* be closed.

We talked it over, and right off it developed that Green was having trouble even getting in to see the proper store officials.

We Start with Number One

O. K., that's Question Number One, all right. So we hammered out a story for Green to use on the prospect's secretary, to get him an appointment. And we worked up a powerful opening that would avoid a brushoff early in the interview. So much for that.

Secondly, we got together some mighty interesting data and statistics to give the prospect pause when he began to say that he wasn't interested in such a deal with *anybody*. You can't argue with figures, you know, if they're accurate and in point and indicate something important.

Third, we found in Green's briefcase some very persuasive materials that showed that his particular outfit was reliable and experienced enough to merit consideration on a proposition of this sort.

Fourth, we drew up a chart that showed all the operating details: amount of space needed, and everything else the store would need to furnish or do, and exactly what his company would do.

"Now I won't get turned down so often on the ground that the store can't spare the space," remarked Green. "I've never had any real answer to that one before."

Five—And You're Safe!

Finally, we built as strong a list as we could of closing arguments, to avoid those indefinite parting remarks like, "Well, Mr. Green, we'll think about it and let you know."

When we were all finished, I said to Jim Green, "Now, remember that 'yes' has 15 letters! And remember that every time you fail to work out a deal, it's got to be because you tripped up on one or more of those five points!"

I happen to know that in the next two months Green got his

full quota—signed up as many stores as his company wanted to take on that year. And if this approach will work on an assignment as tough as his, I think it's pretty clear that it will also work in less complicated circumstances.

Of course, here and there I meet a salesman who thinks his selling problem is outside the scope of what I recommend.

There's Only One Answer

"Tell me," I say under these circumstances, "can you really picture yourself saying 'no' to a salesman, if *you* happened to be the prospect, *except in terms of one or more of those five points?*"

Well, up to now I've never met the man who could talk himself out of that one. Nor do I expect to—ever.

Self-operating Quiz

Do You Really Act on the Following Facts?

1. That every prospect must answer "yes" to five different questions before he can buy? .... Yes_____ No_____

2. That every time a sale is *not* made it's because the prospect failed to answer "yes" to one or more of those five specific questions? .... Yes_____ No_____

3. That the prospect can't be expected to know that *these* questions are involved? Yes_____ No_____

4. That lots of sales are needlessly lost because the salesman tries to sell *his* product before the buyer has agreed that he is open to buy *anyone's?* .... Yes_____ No_____

5. That it's important for the salesman to have a "meeting of the minds" with the prospect as to the *exact composition* of the order before he goes into his final close? .... Yes_____ No_____

6. That it's profitable to plan how you are going to get your five "yes's" before you make each call? .... Yes_____ No_____

7. That it's instructive to determine which of the five evoked a "no" each time you fail to make the sale? .... Yes_____ No_____

8. That keeping a record of such information has helped many a salesman increase his selling strength? .... Yes_____ No_____

9. That you, as a prospect, couldn't fail to place the order except by saying "no" to one or more of these five questions?.... Yes_____ No_____

10. That the principle discussed in this chapter is one of those to which there are *no* exceptions? .... Yes_____ No_____

Your score is _____

If you answered "yes" to only seven (or less) of the ten questions, you need a plan to improve your performance. Think it out and write it out *now*, while you've got it in mind!

18

BROTHER, TELL
THEM!

Bart Cummings is a born story teller. He's got a string of
anecdotes as long as your arm, and they're all good! What's
more, they're all *true*, for Bart has been selling for something
like 20 years, and each of his tales is based on personal experience.

Yes, he'll admit at the drop of a hat that his selling career
has been one long adventure, and there's nothing he'd rather
talk about than the fun, and the hard knocks, that have come
his way.

Of all his stories, there's one that stands out in my mind as
the best. I've often thought to myself, "If there's *one* story that
every salesman should hear, it's Bart's story about how he
licked that slump!"

You Never Can Tell

"You never can tell," Bart would begin, "what tomorrow
may hold in store for you. Like the day my sales manager
asked me if I'd tag along with a new salesman who had just
been trained and was ready to start his field work.

"'Just go along with him, Bart,' he said, 'to help him out if
he works himself into a spot. And you might let me know if
he's got what it takes.'

154

"Well, the truth was that I could hardly afford to waste the day, because my own sales had been anything but good. But what could I do?

"So we started out, this new man and I, and I must admit that my thoughts were on my *own* chances of closing some business within the next few days, rather than on the rough knocks this newcomer might be in for.

"But on our very first interview I got a real jolt! No, we didn't walk out with the order—didn't make a sale till late afternoon, as I recall it. Matter of fact, my companion wasn't

a world-beater, and to make things worse, he wasn't at his best, under the circumstances, that first day.

"There was one thing he did, though, that made me sit up and take notice. He kept dishing out sales points, one after another, until he even had *me* almost excited about our product!

"Now, as I said, he was nervous, and I could tell that even under more favorable circumstances he'd still be a weak closer. But I had sense enough not to let these things blind me to the fact that in one important respect his performance was far better than my own.

Here's the Payoff

"Now, here's the payoff! I realized that I, too, had once used practically every last one of those arguments, and with as much enthusiasm as this lad was displaying now!

"And I guess I must have been a little stronger on the close, for all at once it hit me like a ton of bricks: The really fine record I'd made my first couple of years with the company had been accomplished by a combination of the stuff this chap was handing out, plus a fair amount of selling skill.

"I guess I'll never know just when or why I'd let my presentation go to pot. I do know, however, that far from *wasting* that day, I'd have been ahead of the game if I'd turned my next paycheck over to that kid, because out of that day's experience came the most important thing I know about selling. It's simply this. Just because a sales point has become an old story to *you,* just because here and there you may find a prospect who's already heard it, just because it doesn't always get you the order, don't think for a minute that you can get along without it!

There's Power in This Idea

"But why take my word for it? You can easily find out for yourself how much power there is in this idea, any time you want to.

"For instance, that very evening I spent a couple of hours looking back. I dug up some notes that helped refresh my memory. Right off I ran across a point that, I remembered very well, had gotten me a *lot* of business! Why had I stopped using it? I've no idea; probably it went into the discard when I decided to try a new approach.

"But there's one thing I do know! That day ended my slump! And, what's more, although all this happened more than 15 years ago, nothing that has happened since has lessened my faith in the power of that idea!

The Cart Before the Horse

"Just one thing more before I sign off. The boys often say, 'No wonder Bart tells a story full of punch and packed with reasons-to-buy! Who *wouldn't* be enthusiastic about our line with an income like that!'

"Well, that's the bunk. It's the other way around. I paid the price once for being careless about my presentation—and I don't intend to do it again.

"So, suppose I *have* used an argument a thousand times, suppose it's such an old story to me that way down deep I'd be tickled pink if I could drop it forevermore—for whose benefit is this presentation being made, anyway? For mine or the prospect's? As long as I can tell by the look on his face that *he's* not bored with it, just that long, brother, will I continue to blow my horn!"

Look Out for "Presentation Fatigue"!

Now I've always felt that one of the greatest "occupational hazards" you and I face is the "presentation fatigue" that Bart Cummings referred to.

And how could it be otherwise? You get all zipped up about a new product your company has just brought out. You turn a critical eye on its sales points as you see them after a week's work in the field. "Nice story I've lined up," you tell yourself with some satisfaction.

Well, what happens? You find that on your first trip around

the territory the new product is rather easy to sell. So half your ammunition is stored away as excess baggage, then and there.

But that's not all! You discover in time that *one* of your sales points is rather difficult to explain; another applies only to a certain type of account; a third comes, with constant repetition, to seem so obvious to you that you lose faith in its dramatic value.

We're All Human

Yes, we're all human, and all too often we succumb to these temptations to do, progressively, less and less of an all-out job of using our sales ammunition. And the same thing applies to our efforts to locate new prospects! You've had this experience, I'm sure: You call on a prospect half a dozen times, and nothing happens.

So you decide not to waste any more time on *him*. Then one fine day, you're chagrined to see that he's put in a competing line. "That blasted so-and-so!" you say to yourself. "Why *is* it that people must be so contrary?"

And yet, if only you knew it, the answer may be far removed from contrariness. Maybe it's just that a new salesman in the territory, who hadn't "wised up" to the fact that this man actually *wasn't* a prospect, made the mistake of calling on him at a time when he was ready to be sold!

There Are Three Pitfalls

Yes, the years are inclined to bog us down with presentation fatigue, and prospect fatigue, and product fatigue as well. Sales points and prospects and product features that at first were bright and shiny, gradually but steadily tend to become dull and undramatic.

As this happens, we are spared a record of constantly diminishing sales *only* because there are certain counter-forces. With time, we become more firmly entrenched in our territories and with specific "pet accounts." We grow stronger in many ways, which is of course the way it should be.

But there's a very simple way to measure just how much it costs to let our growing weaknesses act as a drag at the same time that our growing strength entitles us to reach new heights of success.

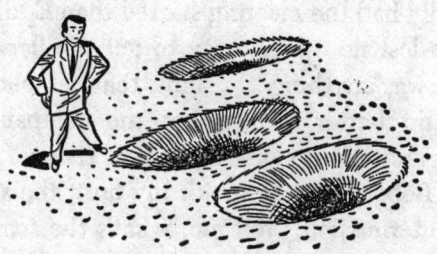

One Man in a Hundred

Just look about you. Yes, just look a bit, until you spot a man who has kept his viewpoint fresh while he was gaining the experience and entrenching his roots and winning the other benefits that time alone can bring.

When you spot him, take off your hat in a well-earned tribute to the one-man-in-a-hundred who has succeeded in escaping the occupational hazard that sooner or later comes to afflict the other 99!

You've never heard of Eddie Prince, I'm sure. But those who

meet him, as I did, are not inclined to forget him soon. It was at a sales meeting that we met, and he was introduced to me not only as the company's *oldest* salesman, but as their representative in an important territory, Chicago.

Eddie Does His Stuff

Well, hardly had the meeting started than Eddie began to do his stuff. He lost no opportunity to get the floor to point out that the line was anything but right; that competition had better prices and better terms; that the company was losing friends right and left because of its policies and practices.

"Tell me, Bob," I pleaded with my host, the sales manager, at the first intermission, "tell me, what's the score on this fellow Prince?"

"That's easy, if you haven't already figured it out," he replied.

"Eddie's been with the company so long that he's built up some very fine accounts. And he lives on them, or should I say 'off them,' day in and day out. But apart from keeping those accounts, he's far and away our poorest salesman, as you have already observed. I stopped long ago expecting him to really work his territory, and he doesn't even do a job of following up on leads that come his way.

Competition Has a Picnic

"We know, of course, that competition is walking away with the business in that territory, except for those old accounts."

I interrupted to agree, "I can understand that, if today's performance reflects his attitude."

"Well," answered my friend, "it's a hard decision to make, but we've very little choice. Next week I'm calling Eddie in for a little talk, to tell him we're putting another man in his territory to call on everyone except his regular accounts."

No, there aren't many men like Eddie Prince, praise the

Lord! Yet in his own way, he serves a useful purpose. For what I see in Eddie Prince is simply this: He represents an extreme case of what we've been discussing. He isn't typical, as I said, but the men who have slipped *half* as far can be counted by the score.

Many Go Half Way

Some men lose half the freshness and vitality of their viewpoint only gradually, in the course of ten or 20 years—or more.

Others lose it faster. Some, like Eddie Prince, manage to lose it all.

But in between, as eloquent testimony to the needlessness of the process, is that superb example of successful salesmanship—the man who retains the ability to hit hard and true in spite of the toll that time and close acquaintance with the job take of so many others.

"He tells his story so effectively that even those who do not need his product wish they *did!*" That is the finest tribute I have ever heard expressed about a salesman. For the man about whom this was said (just like any other man about whom it might be said) had surely and skillfully—and at times, I suppose, painfully—achieved a blend of the new and the old.

Brother, Tell Them!

And this same man, whenever he was asked for advice on selling, always replied, "Brother, *tell them!* They can't know unless you *tell them*. Tell them so that they'll *buy*, and you won't have to worry about *selling* them!"

I think Bart Cummings would agree with that. He learned it the hard way, you may recall. And, as I see it, any salesman who hasn't learned that lesson and learned it *well* stands perilously close to being unsuited to his job.

Self-operating Quiz

Do You Really Act on the Following Facts?

1. That every salesman must guard against letting his presentation grow "rusty" without his realizing it? .... Yes____ No____

2. That we all tend to drop good sales points that have served us well, simply because we ourselves grow tired of using them? .... Yes____ No____

3. That an enthusiastic presentation produces sales, and that it's wrong to say that it's all the sales he's getting that cause a good producer to sound enthusiastic? .... Yes____ No____

4. That a period of easy selling is often the cause of our dropping many good sales points? .... Yes____ No____

5. That the big occupational hazards of salesmanship are presentation fatigue, product fatigue, and prospect fatigue?.. Yes____ No____

6. That a salesman's growing following in his territory often enables him to write enough orders so that he himself doesn't realize that he has succumbed to these occupational hazards? .... Yes____ No____

7. That a man who somehow manages to keep his viewpoint *fresh* while reaping the benefits of being established in his territory is quite exceptional? .... Yes____ No____

8. That the rewards in such exceptional cases are outstanding? .... Yes____ No____

9. That in the course of time some salesmen come to earn their living by selling only established accounts, and completely lose the ability to open new ones?...... Yes____ No____

10. That where that is true, even to a lesser degree, competition has a "field day"?.. Yes____ No____

Your score is _____

If you answered "yes" to only seven (or less) of the ten questions, you need a plan to improve your performance. Think it out and write it out *now*, while you've got it in mind!

19

PUT A "HOOKER" IN YOUR CLOSE!

A Star Is Born

The other day I was having lunch with one of America's most successful sales executives. We were discussing the question of why some salesmen do so much better than others in actually *closing* sales. Finally my companion said, "If you can teach any competent salesman to do just one single thing, you've got a star on your hands. But, first, you've got to teach him how to *put a hooker in every close!*"

Now that may be a new word for you: *Hooker.* But, as I see it, my friend was not exaggerating its importance to any man who earns his living as a salesman.

Let's Look at a Hooker

Perhaps I can explain its meaning in this way. No salesman has ever really made a complete presentation of his offer by merely pointing out *reasons to buy.* No, he hasn't done his job unless and until he points out at least one reason to buy *today!*

Let's examine that proposition with a little care.

Salesman Jones sells home insulation, let's say by way of illustration. He calls on Prospect Smith, and tells a strong story.

164

In due course Smith is convinced that it will be to his advantage to buy. What's more, he's even satisfied that Jones has as good a deal as anybody.

"Now for the close," Jones tells himself, with high expectations.

It Never Fails

Well, if Jones gets that order, you can be sure of one thing. It's that somewhere down the line, perhaps without either party being aware of it, either Jones or his prospect has said or done something that justifies in the prospect's mind making a commitment *today*.

Because, you see, if that hadn't happened, it's a sure-fire bet that Smith, as a normal human being, would have found some reason, or some pretext, for delaying his decision.

And in a minute I think you'll see why this is so. Yes, the key to this all-important matter can be found right in your own behavior when you are a prospect or a buyer.

You need a new car, we'll say, and you have a pretty fair idea of what you want. You've done your share of window-shopping and reading of ads. You have the money to pay for your purchase.

Sure, You're a Prospect

Yes, in anybody's language, at this point you are a prospect.

In due course your car dealer phones. Somehow he's figured out that this might be a good time to buzz you. It is, you admit, and invite him over. He tells his story, and both you and he realize that you have become a very good prospect.

But every time he tries to pin you down, you say, "Well, I don't know. Looks like a good deal, but I want to think about it for a day or two."

Why? It's a million to one that you don't actually realize it but some imp inside you, that streak of normal human nature, is causing you to react that way because there's *nothing in the situation* to make you feel that *this* is a better moment than any *other* to sign on the dotted line!

Here It Comes!

But as you sit there and listen to this salesman point out more features of his product, the telephone rings. Your wife is calling to ask whether Friday night is okay for dinner and cards at the Browns'.

As you hang up, you sense that the whole situation about buying the car has changed. "Be nice to have that new car by Friday," you tell yourself. No, you wouldn't pay $25 extra to have it by then; it doesn't mean that much to you. But you don't have to pay anything extra to get it; all you have to do is say, "O. K., I guess it's a deal. I can pick it up on the way home, you say?"

"Sold" Isn't "Closed"

Do you see what's happened? Five minutes earlier you were really "sold," *yet the salesman couldn't close the deal!* There was just one thing lacking, you see: a hooker!

Now it's obvious that it took only a very minor consideration to fill the bill. Yes, if that salesman had been really smart, he wouldn't have had to be rescued by the sheer coincidence of that phone call. Here's what he would have done, instead.

The Salesman Throws a Hooker

"Mr. Prospect," he would have said, "I'm not going to tell you any more about our car's features, because I think you appreciate them already. But I'll tell you what I'll do. I've got a pretty good idea where I can make a quick sale of your old car that you're going to trade in. If we can close the deal right now, so that I can offer your present car to my prospect right away, I can make you a little more liberal allowance than if you wait a day or two."

Yes, that's smart selling, all right. That little hooker, or any one of a hundred reasons why you should buy *today*, is the difference between a sale made and one postponed.

Well, now you know what a hooker is, but before you're ready to put the idea to work, there are a few more things you'll need to know.

For example, you may be wondering how come, if there's got to be a hooker to close a sale, that so many sales are made by salesmen who don't use them.

Some Prospects Hook Themselves

Now the answer to that one is that in all such cases there *is* a hooker, but it's one that's furnished by the prospect, *not* the salesman.

A typical instance might be the case of a traveling salesman when he calls on either a regular customer or a new account. Maybe not a word is said about it, but the buyer realizes that the salesman is in town only for a few hours, and that fact in itself is a good hooker, because it furnishes a good reason to buy *today* if he wants the line.

Another example would be the case of a vacuum cleaner salesman whose story and demonstration make a good impression. Again it may never be expressed in words, but it so happens that his prospect is about to start her spring cleaning; that fact may be all the hooker that's needed.

Peculiarly enough, the fact that some prospects supply their own hookers has cost untold thousands of lost sales. If *none* of them did, every cub salesman would learn in short order that he must put one in every close or he simply won't make any sales.

But as it is, there's many a man who goes on, year after year, selling those who do part of his job for him, but none of the others.

Two Hookers Are Better Than None!

The answer, of course, is never to rely on your prospect's supplying a reason why he or she should buy today, for two hookers won't do any harm, but *no* hooker means no sale!

Now you might never guess it, but the best hookers in the world are based on *fear*. Yes, fear of losing something of value that you already possess. It's a fascinating story, and I'll give you a few examples of how it works.

You read in the headlines, every so often, that a man or a woman whose house has caught fire dashes back into the burning building to retrieve his or her life's savings. Maybe a thousand dollars that has been carefully hidden in the mattress or the cookie jar.

Well, if you were to ask that same person to go back into that burning inferno, not to retrieve a thousand dollars he *already possesses*, but to win a reward of five times that sum, the chances are you'd be turned down cold.

Now don't ask me why, for I don't know the answer. I do know, however, that that is the way the normal man or woman behaves. They will fight much harder to avoid losing something they *already* own than to *gain* something of greater value that they do *not* own. Similarly, the average person will do something about it if he's threatened with a 10 per cent cut

in pay much more readily and vigorously than if he's told of a way that he can win an increase of twice that amount. And again I say, I don't know why, but that's the way people are.

The smart salesman uses that fact to the full!

Why Not Hit Where It Hurts?

"Your competitor across the street is putting in new sound equipment." There's dynamite in that remark for the salesman trying to sell *his* sound equipment to the motion picture theatre owner or manager. It packs a threat to his established volume of business.

"If you act fast you can avoid . . ." What a hooker *that* one is! Maybe you've been trying to make that sale for a year, or two, or three. Maybe you won't get the order even now.

But you can be sure you've tossed a terrific wallop every time you tempt a prospect to do something that promises to spare him from the loss of something of value he already possesses.

Something for Nothing

Closely related, if not quite so strong, is the normal desire of all of us to get something *extra*, something for nothing. Show your prospect that he can somehow get a better value or a plus consideration if he decides *now* rather than *later*, and, again, you've got yourself a powerful hooker.

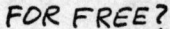

There's one final thing I want to point out to make the picture complete. Once you get the swing of this idea, you'll notice something that I've noticed too, a thousand times. You'll spot salesman after salesman who go right on losing sales they needn't lose, simply because, when the moment comes when you or I would throw a hooker, they go right on stressing *sales points, product features,* or *value.*

It's Always a Mistake

In other words, they make the mistake that the home insulation salesman and the automobile salesman (the ones I told you about before) made. You see, they fail to realize that there's many a prospect who is "sold" but hasn't been *closed.*

He's sold in the sense that he realizes that the particular proposition you've offered him looks good, and that there's no real reason why he shouldn't buy. But—as you know by now—that isn't quite enough. There will be no sale until he feels that there's some reason to buy *today*.

And yet, as I say, these salesmen will go right on adding things that are not needed (reasons to buy) instead of closing the sale by adding the one thing that is needed, (a reason to buy today).

Brother, Get Yourself a Hooker!

Yes, as you spot a salesman making that mistake, you too will wish you could somehow call him aside and say, "Brother, what you need is a *hooker* in that close!"

I hope I've made it clear that hookers don't need to be big or important to do their job. In fact, sometimes the reverse is true. I know a chap who recently went into business for himself. He was naturally eager to open up as many good accounts as he could, so he started out by offering a deal that really amounted to a 10 per cent discount for orders placed at the time of his first call.

Looks Are Deceiving

Now, at first glance you might think that that would be a terrific hooker. But it wasn't! Some buyers were suspicious of a deal of that sort; others thought it was pressure selling. All in all, the deal was a dud.

"Why don't you scale down your deal?" I asked this man when I heard the story.

"Okay! But how?" he countered.

"Well," I replied, "why don't you try out offering your merchandise at regular prices, but telling each prospect that the first store in each neighborhood to buy will be the only one to have your goods as long as they give you a play?"

"Nothing doing on that," he snapped back. "Of course, I wouldn't sell two stores that were real competitors in any case, but that alone won't close sales!"

What Can You Lose?

"Maybe you're right," I conceded, "but we'll never know unless you try it. Your plan isn't working so well. What have you got to lose?"

Now, believe it or not, but the new plan worked like a charm. It was just enough to close the prospects who were already *sold* by the value of the merchandise itself. It was just what was needed!

And so I say, don't think for a minute that using a hooker means pressure selling, or special discounts every time you call, or anything of that sort. No, what's required is a little head-work on your part. Think out in advance of each call what reason you can give to make that particular prospect move from the category of "sold" into the one marked "closed."

You're Better Than You Think!

If you will do that, I think I can promise you a pleasant surprise. Your new sales pace will convince you that all along you've had better values than you ever suspected—that all along you've done a better selling job than even you realized— that all along all you needed to get right up on top was to tell prospects why they should buy *today*.

Yes, you will probably decide that *hooker* is easily the most important word in any salesman's vocabulary, and you'll be dead right!

Self-operating Quiz

Do You Really Act on the Following Facts?

1. That any competent salesman can become a "star" if he will learn how to put a hooker in every close? .... Yes____ No____

2. That there is no really effective method of closing that doesn't include one or more reasons to buy *today?* .... Yes____ No____

3. That no normal, average person will part with his liberty of action unless and until he feels there is some *reason* to make a decision at that time? .... Yes____ No____

4. That every day thousands of prospects are *sold* but not *closed?* .... Yes____ No____

5. That the only reason for this is the lack of a hooker? .... Yes____ No____

6. That a hooker, to be effective, need not be a really *important* reason? .... Yes____ No____

7. That the only reason many salesmen who fail to use hookers succeed in making sales is that under certain circumstances the prospect himself may furnish the necessary hooker? .... Yes____ No____

8. That it's obviously not good salesmanship to depend on it that your prospect will do this part of your job for you?... Yes____ No____

9. That when your prospect is "sold but not closed," it's always a mistake to give him further sales points, since what is needed then is a reason to buy *today?*......... Yes____ No____

10. That a salesman is never ready to make that next call unless he has at least one good hooker ready to use? .... Yes____ No____

Your score is _____

If you answered "yes" to only seven (or less) of the ten questions, you need a plan to improve your performance. Think it out and write it out *now*, while you've got it in mind!

20

YOU'RE ONE UP
ON COMPETITION

Two Miles to Go

Some years ago, while on a motor trip in the Southwest, I somehow got on the wrong road. Like most drivers, I don't like retracing my route, so I kept on going until it became apparent that I was just plain lost.

In due course I came to a crossroads store, and stopped for directions.

"Oklahoma City, eh?" pondered the middle-aged man behind the counter.

"Well," he finally announced, "you keep right on the way you're headed, 'nother 11 miles, till you hit the next town. Then turn left." He carefully indicated the direction.

"Then keep right on that road for quite a spell. Twenty-five miles or more, I'd say. Anyway, you turn left again just two miles before you hit that old iron bridge, and then . . ."

It was difficult for me to keep a straight face, of course, and to refrain from asking him just how I was supposed to know it when I had arrived at the spot called "just two miles before you hit that old iron bridge."

No Meeting of the Minds

Now the thing that has made me remember that conversation is not the humor of the situation. No, I remember it as a rather classic example of how difficult it is for two persons to have a meeting of the minds on even so simple a matter as this one. How difficult it is, in fact, for one man even to convey to another the thought he has in mind!

I often think that it might clarify a lot of things if we were to substitute for the word "sale" the more significant term "meeting of the minds."

Let's Face It

Now I'll admit it might sound strange at first. For example, your sales manager might send out a bulletin, "Jones had eight meetings of the minds last week, for a total of $6,300. That makes him top man for the week, both in dollar volume and in number of meetings of the minds." But, as I said, I think it would put a lot of things in their true light. For me, at least, it puts into sharper focus the exact roles played by both salesman and prospect in this fascinating thing called the selling process.

Now you've often heard it said that in every interview *somebody* makes a sale: Either the salesman convinces the prospect that he should buy, or the prospect convinces the salesman that he can't be sold that day. Just what is it that decides the issue? Why is the "meeting of the minds" sometimes achieved in your favor, and in other cases against you?

A Long Step Forward

Well, I can give you an answer to that one. Although I admit it won't enable you to sell *every* prospect, I think it will take you a long step forward.

And my reason is that, whether we like it or not, it's a fact that every one of us who sells is, in some respect or another, "tough to buy from." Yes, every one of us! The big difference between a star and a dud is pretty much a matter of how tough!

Ed Graham Is Tough

Take Ed Graham, for example. A fine salesman in every respect except one. He's tough to buy from for exactly the same reason as my friend at the crossroads store. Ed's inclined to tell his story in such a way that it's perfectly clear to him, but a way that doesn't fully clarify the matter for the other fellow.

Now Ed doesn't exactly starve to death. He's a hard worker and a strong closer and he means well. He finds enough people who will buy from him in spite of his particular weakness so that he can pay the butcher and the baker. But he'll never really arrive—not so long as he stays that tough to buy from!

How Tough Can a Man Be?

Take the salesman who tried to sell me some new fluorescent lights for my office not long ago. He almost did. I know I tried as hard as I could to buy them!

It all began when I saw an ad that interested me. I called the company, and arranged for this chap to stop in to see me at 4 o'clock. As he told his story I became convinced that here was the solution to my lighting problem.

"Call me Friday about 11, will you? I'll let you know then whether I want them in the chrome finish or plain." The salesman agreed.

But watch what happened next! Instead of phoning as arranged, he *stopped* in to see me on Thursday. Well, I was out of town. He stopped in again on Monday. I was in conference and couldn't be interrupted. He telephoned on Tuesday, about an hour before I was off on a three weeks' trip.

"I Want to Buy"

"I want to buy your equipment, Mr. Black," I told him, "and I want the chrome finish. But I've decided to get your price on our conference room as well as my office. I'm leaving town for several weeks, and will telephone you when I get back, so we can fix this thing up."

Well, I had been back in town almost a month before the thought struck me that I'd not phoned him. Yes, I wanted those lights, and I'm sorry that Mr. Black didn't phone me that Friday at 11, because I was all set to do business that afternoon.

Who's Tough, Anyway?

Now, of course, I don't know, but I wouldn't be surprised if Black thinks I'm hard to sell. Well, for my money, he's hard to buy from.

Let me give you one final example of how this thing works. A large company recently decided to buy about 10,000 electric window signs to give to their retail outlets. I happened to be visiting their sales promotion manager, an old friend of mine.

I was about to leave when he said to me, "If you've a few minutes to spare, I wish you'd wait to see some electric signs we're going to choose from. The salesman has just arrived, and it won't take long." Then he explained that his company did a lot of business with this fellow's outfit, but that he had never met this particular salesman before.

A Good Start

Well, the interview got off to a good start. Bill Todd, my friend, began by saying, "We're wide open as to color, design and so forth. There are only two things we know we want. The sign we select must be suitable for our purpose, and the cost, on an order of ten thousand pieces, must be within $65 per unit."

Now would you believe it? In spite of this guidance, Salesman Morgan spent five valuable minutes extolling the features of a sign which, he then blithely announced, could be bought for a mere $75!

Everybody Goes in Circles

"Price isn't everything, you know," he countered as Todd said that number wouldn't do. And he took three or four minutes more to read a gratuitous lecture on the need to consider value in a deal of this sort.

Well, the upshot was a wasted quarter-hour for each of the three of us. Todd would remind Morgan of price, and Morgan would go right on talking value and features—at prices which in each case were above $65.

Finally Bill Todd said, "Sorry, Mr. Morgan, but I guess you haven't got what we want."

"Well, just a minute, Mr. Todd, I've just had an idea. We do have a sign that might fill your bill, but I still think you'd be better off with this other one."

The Idea Clicks

As he wrote up his order for 2,000 65-dollar signs for a starter, Morgan remarked, "Lucky thing I happened to bring that other number. When I got your message about a 65-dollar sign, I thought you'd probably go a little higher for a better one, but I brought it along—just in case."

Yes, Morgan got his order, but it had been a tough sale, all right.

Who, Me?

There's one thing I'd like to point out right here. Each one of these men I've told you about *thought* he was doing a good job. My friend at the crossroads store? Why, to this day I'll bet he doesn't know that he had failed so completely to put himself in my shoes that his directions were valueless.

Ed Graham, who, as a salesman, had the same difficulty? Ed changed jobs about every two years until he happened to land under a district manager who spotted his difficulty. But Ed couldn't quite see it, so he's still paying the butcher and the baker, but that's all.

And I'll bet Mr. Black, the lighting fixture salesman, will find the going tough until he learns how important it is to keep his dates as agreed. Just like our friend Morgan, until he figures out that his own opinion as to what the buyer should buy may not always be the answer.

Yes, men like these go on missing chances to have a "meeting of the minds" every day in the week.

Yet how easy it is to become "easy to buy from"! None of us can reach perfection, as I said, but every good salesman has somehow learned this lesson. If you think this doesn't mean *you*, let me tell you of one more actual experience that may make you feel otherwise!

Jim Hits the Bumps

There's a man I know—I'll call him Jim Black—who had spent fourteen years in one selling job. His record was average, or a shade better. Then, as the great depression of the thirties got really under way, he found himself "let out."

Weeks of looking and trying finally won him another job. But there was no mistaking one stark fact. Jim had landed a berth that was all straight uphill, and he'd either have to do a minor miracle or make room for a man who could.

Well, a lesser man would have fallen by the wayside. But, in retrospect, it's easy to see that Jim, like so many before and since, found in adversity the turning point to success. He didn't use the same words that I have, about a "meeting of the minds," and "being tough to buy from," but he used exactly the same reasoning. In short, he reached the conclusion that his only chance for success on his new assignment was to whip his own performance into such good shape that he could sell even the tough buyers. You see, that's all he had to work on, now!

Two Years Go By

Two years later Jim accepted an offer to return to his old company, not as a salesman, mind you, but in a post where he could teach others what he had taught himself.

"You're one up on competition," Jim keeps telling all his men. "Yes, you've got competition licked, even if they have a

shade better values, or do more advertising, or have other advantages of that sort. You've got your competitor licked, that is, every time you go about your selling more *intelligently* than he does! And how do you go about doing that? By really putting yourself in your prospect's place!

If You Were the Prospect . . .

"If you were the prospect, would you give the order to a salesman who didn't call on you? No? Then it's only common sense to make all the calls you can each day!

"Or to the man who couldn't tell a story that runs smooth and hits home? Well, then, it's smart to polish up your presentation till it shines.

"Or to the man who falls down in any one of the other dozen ways that any salesman will, if he doesn't keep checking on himself pretty constantly?

"There's Your Answer"

"Well, there's your answer, men. You're either big enough to keep on growing or you're no better than our competitors' salesmen. And there's not much room on this sales force for any man who isn't one up on competition!"

Words That Add Up

Mere words, of course. Words that add up, though, to as fine a selling credo as I ever hope to find. Words that, if put to a fair test by any salesman, instantly open up vast power that must otherwise go untapped.

Yes, as long as there are goods and services to be sold, there will be some men who are "tough to buy from," and they won't be able to sell the prospects who are "tough to sell." And the men who have learned a better way will continue to stand out like bright stars on a dark night.

SELF-OPERATING QUIZ

Do You Really Act on the Following Facts?

1. That it's difficult for one person to convey even a simple idea to another with a high degree of accuracy and completeness? .... Yes____ No____

2. That a sale is really a "meeting of the minds"? .... Yes____ No____

3. That every salesman is, in some respect, "tough to buy from"? .... Yes____ No____

4. That the difference between a "star" and a "dud" is: It's a lot tougher to buy from the latter than from the former? .... Yes____ No____

5. That selling that has more than average intelligence behind it always puts the salesman "one up on competition" even if competition offers better value, or some other advantage? .... Yes____ No____

6. That the best way of placing oneself one up on the competition is to find the means to "put yourself in your prospect's place"? .... Yes____ No____

7. That it's often tough sledding that impels a salesman to take stock of himself in such a way that he succeeds in finding out where there is room for improvement in his performance? .... Yes____ No____

8. That a salesman who isn't big enough to keep on growing is slipping? .... Yes____ No____

9. That you can't grow once you cease to have an open mind as to new ideas, better methods, and suggestions? .... Yes____ No____

10. That a salesman who can't name those things he must "watch" hasn't done enough thinking about his own selling pattern? .... Yes____ No____

Your score is _____

If you answered "yes" to only seven (or less) of the ten questions, you need a plan to improve your performance. Think it out and write it out *now*, while you've got it in mind!

21

SALESMAN'S
TROUBLE SHOOTER

This is a very practical working tool, not a gadget or a novelty.

It will not *teach* you how to sell. It will, however, *remind* you of the particular tools you need to use to solve a particular sales problem.

The Trouble Shooter is divided into six sections, as follows:

1. Closing
2. Objections
3. Your Presentation
4. How to Find Prospects
5. How to Lick a Slump
6. Checklist of Good Selling Habits

Here's how to use the Trouble Shooter. Whenever you run into tough selling, or whenever your next call requires or justifies special preparation, simply turn to the section or sections that appear to *mesh* with your needs. If necessary, continue to read in *other* sections of the Trouble Shooter until you find that you are equipped to handle the situation.

But remember that the Trouble Shooter is too compact to *explain* or *illustrate* each point. Its function is to *remind* you of points that are *explained elsewhere* in this book.

If you want a quick approach to *explanatory* material on some particular point, turn to the following chapter (Chapter 22), entitled Finder for Review.

CLOSING

A. Closing is the *most* important thing in selling.
B. Closing is practically every salesman's *weakest point.*
C. But, good closing *can* be learned!

Rule 1

Close early; close late; close often! Don't be afraid of a "no"; keep right on with your story and *close again soon,* and again and again.

This is the famous method of *trial closing.* Follow this rule and sooner or later you'll undoubtedly hit the right spot for a close that will *make the sale.*

Warning: "one-shot" closing technique is *always* a mistake.

Rule 2

Use *tested methods* of closing for your trial closes:

(a) Try to get agreement on a minor point ("Would you want this in red or in blue?" or "Shall we ship by express or by parcel post?" and so forth).

(b) Assume you've made the sale (start writing the order; or say, "Suppose we send you the larger model; I guess that's the one you want, isn't it?" and so on).

(c) Ask "closing-minded" questions ("Is there anything you're in doubt about, Mr. Jones?" or, "Why don't you let me send this on?").

Rule 3

Learn and *use* the principle of the *hooker.* Always state some reason why it will be to your prospect's advantage to give you the order *today.*

Examples

"If you buy today, you will have this merchandise in stock *before* your competitors do."

"Our assortment is much more complete now than it will be even a *little* later."

"We have a special offer at this time."

"If you give me the order now, I can give you 30 days' extra dating."

Only *you* can decide what hookers apply to your business. You can *always* find some reason why it will be advantageous to buy *today*. If you can't find such a reason, keep on thinking till you do. Remember: There are always one or more hookers for you to use. Find them!

Rule 4

The minute you get into a close that clicks, *stop talking* and write up that order!

Hundreds of sales are killed every hour of the day because the salesman continues to sell *after* the prospect has decided to buy!

Rule 5

As soon as you properly can after the sale is made, *get out!* Don't invite reconsideration once the decision is made in your favor!

OBJECTIONS

Rule 1

You can actually *capitalize* almost any objection that is tossed at you.

Objection: "Your price is too high."

Answer: "Yes, we are the highest-priced in our field, yet we do 6 million dollars a year at these same prices. We couldn't do that if our values weren't mighty fine, could we?"

Objection: "We've been buying from the Jones Company for 20 years, and are completely satisfied."

Answer: "Oh, I know that! And I'd be wasting your time and mine, under the circumstances, if I *didn't have something so attractive* to offer you that it will *overcome that disadvantage!*"

Rule 2

If you know an objection exits, capitalize it even *before* your prospect has a chance to use it.

Example

"Mr. Smith, I know you've been buying from the Jones Company for 20 years, and are completely satisfied. Now I'd be wasting your time and mine, under the circumstances, *if I didn't have something so attractive* to offer you that it will *overcome that disadvantage!*"

Rule 3

If your prospect has an objection in mind, you must get it out in the open. If you don't, you'll lose the sale; if you *do,* you can almost always *kill* the objection.

Example

"Mr. Prospect, are you hesitating because you think prices may drop?"

"Well, yes! That's what's bothering me!"

"O. K., now here's why we are quite certain prices will not go down this year."

Or, "O. K., here's how we will protect you," and so forth.

You *can't* make the sale unless you lick the objection. You *can't* lick the objection unless you get it *out in the open.*

Rule 4

Never confuse an *excuse* with a real *objection.* An excuse is designed to "brush you off" without revealing what's *really* on the prospect's mind. Excuses should be *evaded;* objections should be *met.*

Example

"I won't give you the order, because I don't like the way your company has cut down its advertising allowance."

"Mr. Customer, I'd like to discuss that with you in a minute, but first let me tell you about our line for the new season."

Rule 5

Never, never, *never* treat as an objection or as an excuse a statement that really is a signal that you've made a sale!

Example

"Well, Mr. Salesman, I don't suppose I really *should* spend quite that much money."

Or, "I guess it would be smart for me to wait till my partner gets back to town next week."

Sure, these *sound* like objections, but if you examine them carefully you'll see that they are really "buying signals." Your prospect is sold, and he needs only a little reassurance that he's doing the *right* thing. *Don't kill the sale* by treating a buying signal like an objection. Just say, quietly and slowly, "I'm sure you'll be more than satisfied with this deal, Mr. Prospect. Now if you'll just sign here. . . ."

YOUR PRESENTATION

Remember that when a prospect lets you tell your story, that's your *big moment*. Make the most of it by being fully *prepared*.

Rule 1

Always state, in the first few sentences, a reason for your call.

Wrong: "Mr. Prospect, I happened to be in the neighborhood, so I thought I'd drop in."

Right: "Mr. Prospect, I have a very special reason for calling on *you* today."

In this way you make your call seem *important*, not casual.

Rule 2

Build your talk around buying motives; they are the salesman's best friend.

Buying motives are your prospect's expectation of gain.

What does your prospect *want* to gain? Money? Then show him how *your offer* will make money for him.

Prestige? Then show how *your offer* will add to his prestige.

Security? Then show how *your offer* will help him avoid risks, uncertainty, and the like.

Best buying motives are:

Money
Security
Health
Popularity, prestige, and the like
Less worry
Less work.

So emphasize what your product or service will *do* for him, not why it's good.

Wrong: "This widget is made of solid brass."

Right: "This widget will outlast three of any other make; it's solid brass."

Wrong: "We are the world's largest manufacturers of this type of machine."

Right: "Because we are the world's largest manufacturers of this type of machine, we have lower prices than anyone else."

Rule 3

"Close" *frequently* in your presentation; you never know how soon your prospect may be ready to say "O. K."

Rule 4

Make your presentation so clear that a 15-year-old boy would be certain to understand you. If you don't, you won't make many sales!

Rule 5

Be *specific*. Avoid generalities as you would poison! Master this rule and watch your sales soar!

How to Find Prospects

Rule 1

Unless your product is definitely a non-repeat item, you can be sure that your best prospects are those who have already bought. Sell them more; sell them other items; sell them accessories; sell them new models or bigger models.

Rule 2

Surest way to put Rule 1 into effect is to think out how you can increase the use, consumption, or resale (as the case may be) of your products.

Don't sell these two rules short! Previous buyer plus salesman's ingenuity add up to a formula that can't be beat!

Rule 3

As long as there is such a thing as selling there will be rich rewards in cold turkey prospecting. There is no surer way of making sales than to *open doors*. Even a *weak* salesman can make the grade if he'll follow this rule. Sure, it takes grit. But it never fails. Never!

Rule 4

Keep your records straight. Don't kid yourself that you'll make the callbacks you should if you rely on your memory. Which is better, a sloppy record system, or a pocket full of orders? You can't have both!

Rule 5

Force yourself to call back two or three times on that tough prospect who "gave you the gate." Remember that most tough prospects are much more changeable than those who give a man a fair hearing. Maybe you'll catch him in an entirely different mood today!

How to Lick a Slump

Rule 1

There are five, and only five, ways that *any* salesman can raise his score:

(a) *Close* a greater percentage of the prospects you call on.

(b) *Call on* more prospects per day; then, even with your *same* percentage of closing, you'll get more volume.

(c) Sell *more* units on each sale.

(d) Sell *higher priced* units.

(e) Sell your line "across the board"; that is, sell *all* your products to every customer, wherever possible.

Remember, there *is* no way to increase sales except by these five means, so think hard how you can best use each one of them.

Rule 2

Avoid "peak-and-valley" selling. Only a second-rate salesman makes the mistake of putting all his eggs in one basket by concentrating on one, or a few, big deals or prospects.

A topflight salesman gets his share of big sales, but he gets on top and stays on top by selling lots of bread-and-butter orders too. Thus, if a big deal falls through, he still has a good score. This is the *most important rule* in the whole game of selling.

Rule 3

Make sure that *you* are not "tough to buy from." Most salesmen are. Check yourself. Are *you* guilty of: Too few calls per day? "Fuzzy" presentation instead of a really smooth one? Lack of planning? (If you waited until today to plan today's work, don't kid yourself that you *plan* your work.) Lack of full product information? Lack of *tested* answers to *all* objections you meet in your work?

Rule 4

Finally, if these three rules don't show you the way out of your slump, take these two further steps:

(a) Turn to "Checklist of Good Selling Habits." Consider each point carefully. Be fair. Remember that if you're not doing a real selling job, the reason (or reasons) must show up in the checklist.

(b) Then turn to the beginning and work through to the end of this Salesman's Trouble Shooter.

Important: Why *should* you go over all this material, which you have already read *before?*

That's a good question. Here's the answer: The Trouble Shooter is unique. In a few, compact paragraphs it lists all the things that the experiences of thousands of salesmen show are essential for sales success. Because it is compact, it doesn't go into detail. Result: Each time you read it, you get additional "slants" that you may have missed before. Slumps can't stand up under brainsweat. This Trouble Shooter is a brainsweat stimulator. It won't help you if you play with it like a toy!

CHECKLIST OF GOOD SELLING HABITS

Note: All references in parentheses below are to other parts of this chapter.

Check yourself periodically, especially when the going is tough, on the following:

1. Making enough calls per day?
2. Doing enough "cold-turkey" prospecting? (*See* "How to Find Prospects," Rule 3.)
3. Feeling fit, mentally and physically?
4. Appearance good?
5. Annoying or distracting mannerisms eliminated?
6. Using a smooth, powerful *tested* sales presentation? (*See* "Your Presentation.")

7. Reviewed all your product information *recently?* (We all forget!)
8. Ready with a real answer for every objection you've met? (Practically every objection can actually be *capitalized!*) (*See* "Objections," Rule 1.)
9. Keeping proper records? (*See* "How to Find Prospects," Rule 4.)
10. Avoiding "peak-and-valley" selling by selling enough "bread-and-butter" orders so that you're not out on a limb if your "big" prospects fall down? (*See* "How to Lick a Slump," Rule 2.)
11. Appealing to "buying motives"? (*See* "Your Presentation," Rule 2.)
12. Invariably plan tomorrow's work *today?*
13. Putting a "hooker" in your close? (*See* "Closing," Rule 3.)
14. Really strong on the close? (*See* "Closing," Rules 1 to 5.)
15. Always open up with a "reason for call"? (*See* "Your Presentation," Rule 1.)
16. Feel that your territory isn't right, or anything that *might* be an alibi?
17. Relations with "The House" good? Does everybody in the organization think you're "one swell guy" (and therefore go out of his way to work with you)? There's plenty of power in this idea!

Important: Remind yourself frequently that the greatest occupational hazard in selling is that when the going gets tough the salesman may forget that

(a) "A salesman is a man who *sells*" (not a man who can explain *why* he isn't selling, or one who can point to prospects he's warming up, and so forth);

(b) The "star" has somehow managed to lick tough territory, tough prospects, tough breaks, and other obstacles, whereas the second-rater uses these as an alibi because he really has come to believe that his assignment is tougher than the other man's.

If you don't "feel in your bones" the common senses basis of these two points, or if you think your case is an exception, you can be certain that your sales-ignition system is on the blink. Get it fixed if you expect to get anywhere.

22

FINDER FOR REVIEW

Any material on salesmanship that has proved sound and worth while on first acquaintance is good material to *review* from time to time.

This book is so arranged that it can conveniently be reviewed in three different ways, depending upon your circumstances and needs.

First, you can reread the entire work. If the experience of others is a sound guide, you will derive even more from your rereading than you did from your first trip through.

Second, the Salesman's Trouble Shooter (Chapter 21) enables you to review *in outline form* the particular tools needed to solve particular selling problems.

But there are many occasions when a still different approach is required. Suppose you don't have the several hours required to reread this book from cover to cover, yet you want *more* than the reminder outline that appears in the preceding chapter (Chapter 21). In such a case, this is the chapter you should turn to.

Here you will find a completely different approach to your problem. Experience teaches that there are 13 different "stumbling blocks" that commonly confront the salesman. Not that you, or any other salesman, are troubled by *all* of these at any one time! Quite the contrary; you are much more likely to find yourself saying, "If only I could do a better job of *closing!*" Or of getting the interview. Or of meeting objections.

Because we think of our problems in this purely functional way, this chapter is designed on a purely functional pattern. Simply read the headings of the 13 categories that appear below, select the one (or perhaps two) that represent your problem, and then read the material there indicated.

You will note that you are referred to chapters, not to specific pages. This means that there is something worth reviewing on your particular point in the chapter referred to, and since each of the chapters is brief, you will want to run through it, rather than to "pick up" somewhere in the middle.

One thing more. Because, on a *functional* basis, "closing" and "meeting objections" are very closely related, you will be referred to the material on *both*, regardless of which reference you begin with. Just a little imagination will help you find the ideas you need, even if they do not refer to your specific problem by name.

SUBJECT	CHAPTER
1. Closing	3, 4, 17, 19, 9, 11, 13, 16, 18
2. Getting the Interview	3, 9, 17, 18, 19
3. Objections	3, 4, 6, 9, 10, 15, 16, 17, 19
4. Your Presentation	8, 18, 3, 4, 5, 6, 9, 10, 11, 15, 16, 17, 19, 20
5. Planning Your Work	5, 7, 11, 13, 14, 15, 16, 17, 18, 20
6. Knowing Your Product	16, 5, 6, 15, 18
7. Meeting Competition	5, 6, 9, 10, 15, 16, 18, 20
8. Finding Prospects	5, 7, 13, 15, 16
9. Finding Sales Points	6, 7, 15, 16, 19
10. Buying Motives	6, 19, 7, 15, 16, 17
11. Developing Sales Ideas	13, 16, 17, 19
12. Handling Complaints	9, 17
13. Buying Signals	10, 19

INDEX

197